INVESTIGATIONS IN NUMBER, DATA, AND SPACE®

2-D Geometry

Flips, Turns, and Area

Grade 3

Also appropriate for Grade 4

Douglas H. Clements
Susan Jo Russell
Cornelia Tierney
Michael T. Battista
Julie Sarama Meredith

Developed at TERC, Cambridge, Massachusetts

Dale Seymour Publications®
Menlo Park, California

The *Investigations* curriculum was developed at TERC (formerly Technical Education Research Centers) in collaboration with Kent State University and the State University of New York at Buffalo. The work was supported in part by National Science Foundation Grant No. ESI-9050210. TERC is a nonprofit company working to improve mathematics and science education. TERC is located at 2067 Massachusetts Avenue, Cambridge, MA 02140.

This project was supported, in part,
by the
National Science Foundation
Opinions expressed are those of the authors
and not necessarily those of the Foundation

Managing Editor: Catherine Anderson
Series Editor: Beverly Cory
Revision Team: Laura Marshall Alavosus, Ellen Harding, Patty Green Holubar, Suzanne Knott, Beverly Hersh Lozoff
ESL Consultant: Nancy Sokol Green
Production/Manufacturing Director: Janet Yearian
Production/Manufacturing Coordinator: Barbara Atmore
Design Manager: Jeff Kelly
Design: Don Taka
Illustrations: Jane McCreary, Carl Yoshihara
Cover: Bay Graphics
Composition: Archetype Book Composition

This book is published by Dale Seymour Publications®, an imprint of Addison Wesley Longman, Inc.

Dale Seymour Publications
2725 Sand Hill Road
Menlo Park, CA 94025
Customer Service: 800-872-1100

Order number DS43843
ISBN 1-57232-696-4
2 3 4 5 6 7 8 9 10-ML-01 00 99 98

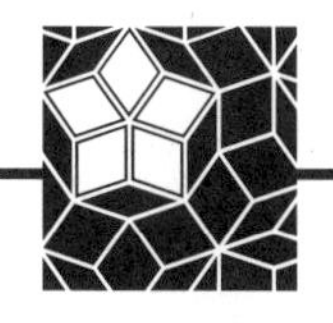

TERC

INVESTIGATIONS IN NUMBER, DATA, AND SPACE®

Principal Investigator **Susan Jo Russell**

Co-Principal Investigator **Cornelia C. Tierney**

Director of Research and Evaluation **Jan Mokros**

Curriculum Development

Joan Akers
Michael T. Battista
Mary Berle-Carman
Douglas H. Clements
Karen Economopoulos
Ricardo Nemirovsky
Andee Rubin
Susan Jo Russell
Cornelia C. Tierney
Amy Shulman Weinberg

Evaluation and Assessment

Mary Berle-Carman
Abouali Farmanfarmaian
Jan Mokros
Mark Ogonowski
Amy Shulman Weinberg
Tracey Wright
Lisa Yaffee

Teacher Development and Support

Rebecca B. Corwin
Karen Economopoulos
Tracey Wright
Lisa Yaffee

Technology Development

Michael T. Battista
Douglas H. Clements
Julie Sarama Meredith
Andee Rubin

Video Production

David A. Smith

Administration and Production

Amy Catlin
Amy Taber

Cooperating Classrooms for This Unit

Katie Bloomfield
Robert A. Dihlmann
Shutesbury Elementary
Shutesbury, MA

Sharon Cacicia
Janice Wagner
Starpoint Central Schools
Lockport, NY

Sharon Freeze
Williamsville Central Schools
Williamsville, NY

Joyce Golibersuch
Sue Combs
Buffalo Public Schools
Buffalo, NY

Corrine Varon
Virginia M. Micciche
Cambridge Public Schools
Cambridge, MA

Jeanne Wall
Arlington Public Schools
Arlington, MA

Consultants and Advisors

Elizabeth Badger
Deborah Lowenberg Ball
Marilyn Burns
Ann Grady
Joanne M. Gurry
James J. Kaput
Steven Leinwand
Mary M. Lindquist
David S. Moore
John Olive
Leslie P. Steffe
Peter Sullivan
Grayson Wheatley
Virginia Woolley
Anne Zarinnia

Graduate Assistants

Kent State University
Joanne Caniglia
Pam DeLong
Carol King

State University of New York at Buffalo
Rosa Gonzalez
Sue McMillen
Julie Sarama Meredith
Sudha Swaminathan

Revisions and Home Materials

Cathy Miles Grant
Marlene Kliman
Margaret McGaffigan
Megan Murray
Kim O'Neil
Andee Rubin
Susan Jo Russell
Lisa Seyferth
Myriam Steinback
Judy Storeygard
Anna Suarez
Cornelia Tierney
Carol Walker
Tracey Wright

CONTENTS

TEACHER NOTES

WHERE TO START

The first-time user of *Flips, Turns, and Area* should read the following:

When you next teach this same unit, you can begin to read more of the background. Each time you present the unit, you will learn more about how your students understand the mathematical ideas.

ABOUT THE *INVESTIGATIONS* CURRICULUM

Investigations in Number, Data, and Space® is a K–5 mathematics curriculum with four major goals:

- to offer students meaningful mathematical problems
- to emphasize depth in mathematical thinking rather than superficial exposure to a series of fragmented topics
- to communicate mathematics content and pedagogy to teachers
- to substantially expand the pool of mathematically literate students

The *Investigations* curriculum embodies a new approach based on years of research about how children learn mathematics. Each grade level consists of a set of separate units, each offering 2–8 weeks of work. These units of study are presented through investigations that involve students in the exploration of major mathematical ideas.

Approaching the mathematics content through investigations helps students develop flexibility and confidence in approaching problems, fluency in using mathematical skills and tools to solve problems, and proficiency in evaluating their solutions. Students also build a repertoire of ways to communicate about their mathematical thinking, while their enjoyment and appreciation of mathematics grows.

The investigations are carefully designed to invite all students into mathematics—girls and boys, members of diverse cultural, ethnic, and language groups, and students with different strengths and interests. Problem contexts often call on students to share experiences from their family, culture, or community. The curriculum eliminates barriers—such as work in isolation from peers, or emphasis on speed and memorization—that exclude some students from participating successfully in mathematics. The following aspects of the curriculum ensure that all students are included in significant mathematics learning:

- Students spend time exploring problems in depth.
- They find more than one solution to many of the problems they work on.
- They invent their own strategies and approaches, rather than relying on memorized procedures.
- They choose from a variety of concrete materials and appropriate technology, including calculators, as a natural part of their everyday mathematical work.
- They express their mathematical thinking through drawing, writing, and talking.
- They work in a variety of groupings—as a whole class, individually, in pairs, and in small groups.
- They move around the classroom as they explore the mathematics in their environment and talk with their peers.

While reading and other language activities are typically given a great deal of time and emphasis in elementary classrooms, mathematics often does not get the time it needs. If students are to experience mathematics in depth, they must have enough time to become engaged in real mathematical problems. We believe that a minimum of five hours of mathematics classroom time a week—about an hour a day—is critical at the elementary level. The plan and pacing of the *Investigations* curriculum is based on that belief.

We explain more about the pedagogy and principles that underlie these investigations in Teacher Notes throughout the units. For correlations of the curriculum to the NCTM Standards and further help in using this research-based program for teaching mathematics, see the following books:

- *Implementing the* Investigations in Number, Data, and Space® *Curriculum*
- *Beyond Arithmetic: Changing Mathematics in the Elementary Classroom* by Jan Mokros, Susan Jo Russell, and Karen Economopoulos

This book is one of the curriculum units for *Investigations in Number, Data, and Space.* In addition to providing part of a complete mathematics curriculum for your students, this unit offers information to support your own professional development. You, the teacher, are the person who will make this curriculum come alive in the classroom; the book for each unit is your main support system.

Although the curriculum does not include student textbooks, reproducible sheets for student work are provided in the unit and are also available as Student Activity Booklets. Students work actively with objects and experiences in their own environment and with a variety of manipulative materials and technology, rather than with a book of instruction and problems. We strongly recommend use of the overhead projector as a way to present problems, to focus group discussion, and to help students share ideas and strategies.

Ultimately, every teacher will use these investigations in ways that make sense for his or her particular style, the particular group of students, and the constraints and supports of a particular school environment. Each unit offers information and guidance for a wide variety of situations, drawn from our collaborations with many teachers and students over many years. Our goal in this book is to help you, a professional educator, implement this curriculum in a way that will give all your students access to mathematical power.

Investigation Format

The opening two pages of each investigation help you get ready for the work that follows.

What Happens This gives a synopsis of each session or block of sessions.

Mathematical Emphasis This lists the most important ideas and processes students will encounter in this investigation.

What to Plan Ahead of Time These lists alert you to materials to gather, sheets to duplicate, transparencies to make, and anything else you need to do before starting.

INVESTIGATION 1

Motions with Tetrominoes

What Happens

Session 1: Tetrominoes Students find all possible arrangements of four squares, called *tetrominoes*. They use informal language to describe the motions they can use to overlay two shapes for comparison, to convince someone that one shape is or is not the same as another. They use a single tetromino repeatedly to make a pattern that will cover a 10-by-12 grid of squares.

Sessions 2 and 3: Slides, Flips, and Turns Students continue to explore how they can cover an area with tetrominoes. In the computer game, Tumbling Tetrominoes, they practice the three basic geometric motions—slides, flips, and turns. There are two class discussions, one about the off-computer activity, one about the computer game; you will decide the best time to hold these, depending on when students have had enough experience with the activity to reflect on the discussion questions.

Session 4: Rectangles with Different Shapes Students construct different-shaped rectangles with the same area, cutting apart 10-by-12 grids and reassembling the pieces into new rectangles. Students also work on the computer game, Tumbling Tetrominoes, with different-shaped rectangles. They discuss the "fairness" of the different shapes, touching on ideas about conservation of area and strategies for covering.

Session 5: Final Challenges Students cover their different-shaped rectangles with tetrominoes and explore whether the same tetrominoes can cover these new rectangles as covered the original 10-by-12 grid. In the computer game, students are challenged to try the Star level, in which they cannot erase a move or flip the given shapes. As an assessment, students complete a puzzle that requires them to visualize the motions they've been using.

Mathematical Emphasis

- Measuring area by covering a flat space with square units
- Finding systematically all possible geometric arrangements of a given number of squares
- Finding patterns for covering a space
- Comparing areas of rectangles with different dimensions
- Describing physical motions in precise ways as a series of slides, flips, and turns
- Comparing two shapes to decide if they are congruent or not after using geometric motions—slides, flips, and turns—to try fitting one shape exactly on top of the other

2 ▪ *Investigation 1: Motions with Tetrominoes*

INVESTIGATION 1

What to Plan Ahead of Time

Materials

- Interlocking cubes: 130 per pair (Sessions 1–3)
- Resealable plastic bags or envelopes: 1 per student (Session 1)
- Overhead projector, transparencies and pens (Sessions 1–2)
- Scissors, crayons, glue (Sessions 2–3, 5)
- Apple Macintosh disk, Tumbling Tetrominoes, for *Flips, Turns, and Area* (Sessions 2–5)
- Computers (Macintosh II or above) with 4 MB of internal memory (RAM) and Apple System Software 7.0 or later: 1 per pair (Sessions 2–5)
- Standard number cubes and crayons or markers (Sessions 2–3, optional)
- Transparent or masking tape (Session 4)

Other Preparation

- If you plan to provide folders in which students will save their work for the entire unit, prepare these for distribution during Session 1.
- Try to make the set of tetrominoes yourself; see the **Teacher Note**, What's an –Omino? (p. 8) for directions. (Session 1)
- Use the disk for *Flips, Turns, and Area* to install the game Tumbling Tetrominoes on each available computer (see p. 57). Try the Tumbling Tetrominoes game. (Session 2)
- If you have fewer than the recommended computers, or none at all, see the **Teacher Note**, Managing the Computer Activities (p. 9), for alternative ways to present the unit. (Session 2)
- Prepare a 5-by-24 grid for each pair of students by cutting the 10-by-12 Rectangle (p. 75) in half lengthwise and taping the short ends together. (Session 5)
- Duplicate student sheets and teaching resources (located at the end of this unit) in the following quantities. If you have Student Activity Booklets, copy only the items marked with an asterisk, including any transparencies needed.

For all sessions

10-by-12 Rectangle (p. 75): at least 11 per student, and 1 transparency.* **Note:** This grid is used throughout the investigation for many purposes. The quantity needed will vary with your classroom and the choices you make; plan to make more copies as needed.

For Session 1

Student Sheet 1, Making Tetrominoes (p. 61): 1 per student (homework)

Family letter* (p. 60): 1 per student. Remember to sign it before copying.

For Sessions 2–3

Student Sheet 2, How to Play Tumbling Tetrominoes (p. 62): 1 per pair, or 1 per computer

Student Sheet 3, Game Records (p. 64): 1 per pair

Student Sheet 4, The Perfect Cover-Up (p. 65): 1 per student (homework)

Student Sheet 5, How Many Squares? (p. 66): 1 per student (homework)

For Session 5

Student Sheet 6, Puzzle Pieces (p. 67): 1 per student

Investigation 1: Motions with Tetrominoes ▪ 3

Sessions Within an investigation, the activities are organized by class session, a session being at least a one-hour math class. Sessions are numbered consecutively through an investigation. Often several sessions are grouped together, presenting a block of activities with a single major focus.

When you find a block of sessions presented together—for example, Sessions 1, 2, and 3—read through the entire block first to understand the overall flow and sequence of the activities. Make some preliminary decisions about how you will divide the activities into three sessions for your class, based on what you know about your students. You may need to modify your initial plans as you progress through the activities, and you may want to make notes in the margins of the pages as reminders for the next time you use the unit.

Be sure to read the Session Follow-Up section at the end of the session block to see what homework assignments and extensions are suggested as you make your initial plans.

While you may be used to a curriculum that tells you exactly what each class session should cover, we have found that the teacher is in a better position to make these decisions. Each unit is flexible and may be handled somewhat differently by every teacher. While we provide guidance for how many sessions a particular group of activities is likely to need, we want you to be active in determining an appropriate pace and the best transition points for your class. It is not unusual for a teacher to spend more or less time than is proposed for the activities.

Ten-Minute Math At the beginning of some sessions, you will find Ten-Minute Math activities. These are designed to be used in tandem with the investigations, but not during the math hour. Rather, we hope you will do them whenever you have a spare 10 minutes—maybe before lunch or recess, or at the end of the day.

Ten-Minute Math offers practice in key concepts, but not always those being covered in the unit. For example, in a unit on using data, Ten-Minute Math might revisit geometric activities done earlier in the year. Complete directions for the suggested activities are included at the end of each unit.

Sessions 2 and 3

Slides, Flips, and Turns

Materials

- Interlocking cubes (130 per pair)
- Students' envelopes of tetrominoes
- 10-by-12 Rectangle (1–6 per student)
- Scissors, crayons, glue (optional)
- Computers with Tumbling Tetrominoes installed
- Student Sheet 2 (1 per computer)
- Student Sheet 3 (1 per pair)
- Student Sheet 4 (1 per student, homework)
- Student Sheet 5 (1 per student, homework)

For the paper version of Tumbling Tetrominoes:

- 10-by-12 Rectangle (1 per student)
- One standard number cube
- Crayons or markers

What Happens

Students continue to explore how they can cover an area with tetrominoes. In the computer game, Tumbling Tetrominoes, they practice the three basic geometric motions—slides, flips, and turns. There are two class discussions, one about the off-computer activity, one about the computer game; you will decide the best time to hold these, depending on when students have had enough experience with the activity to reflect on the discussion questions. Their work focuses on:

- covering a rectangular region with tetrominoes of a single shape, looking for patterns and larger units
- forming conjectures as to why certain tetrominoes will cover the region completely and some will not
- giving explicit commands—slides, flips, and turns—to the computer to move tetrominoes to completely cover a rectangular region
- visualizing how one shape can be moved to best fit into a spatial arrangement of shapes

Ten-Minute Math: Broken Calculator Two or three times during Investigation 1, in a spare 10 minutes any time during your class day, use the activity Broken Calculator. This activity gives students practice in solving computation problems flexibly.

Pose problems like these:

Put 125 on your calculator screen without pressing 1 or 5.

Add 62 and 30 without pressing 3.

Add 48 and 48 without pressing 4 or 8.

After students solve the problem, list some of their solutions on the board. Ask students to choose one solution and extend it into a series that follows a pattern. For example, to form 125 without pressing 1 or 5:

$99 + 24 + 2 = 125$
$98 + 24 + 3 = 125$
$97 + 24 + 4 = 125$

For full directions and variations, see p. 53.

10 ■ *Investigation 1: Motions with Tetrominoes*

Activities The activities include pair and small-group work, individual tasks, and whole-class discussions. In any case, students are seated together, talking and sharing ideas during all work times. Students most often work cooperatively, although each student may record work individually.

Choice Time In some units, some sessions are structured with activity choices. In these cases, students may work simultaneously on different activities focused on the same mathematical ideas. Students choose which activities they want to do, and they cycle through them.

You will need to decide how to set up and introduce these activities and how to let students make their choices. Some teachers present them as station activities, in different parts of the room. Some list the choices on the board as reminders or have students keep their own lists.

Extensions Sometimes in Session Follow-Up, you will find suggested extension activities. These are opportunities for some or all students to explore a topic in greater depth or in a different context. They are not designed for "fast" students; mathematics is a multifaceted discipline, and different students will want to go further in different investigations. Look for and encourage the sparks of interest and enthusiasm you see in your students, and use the extensions to help them pursue these interests.

Excursions Some of the *Investigations* units include excursions—blocks of activities that could be omitted without harming the integrity of the unit. This is one way of dealing with the great depth and variety of elementary mathematics—much more than a class has time to explore in any one year. Excursions give you the flexibility to make different choices from year to year, doing the excursion in one unit this time, and next year trying another excursion.

Tips for the Linguistically Diverse Classroom I-15

At strategic points in each unit, you will find concrete suggestions for simple modifications of the teaching strategies to encourage the participation of all students. Many of these tips offer alternative ways to elicit critical thinking from students at varying levels of English proficiency, as well as from other students who find it difficult to verbalize their thinking.

The tips are supported by suggestions for specific vocabulary work to help ensure that all students can participate fully in the investigations. The Preview for the Linguistically Diverse Classroom (p. I-18) lists important words that are assumed as part of the working vocabulary of the unit. Second-language learners will need to become familiar with these words in order to understand the problems and activities they will be doing. These terms can be incorporated into students' second-language work before or during the unit. Activities that can be used to present the words are found in the appendix, Vocabulary Support for Second-Language Learners (p. 55). In addition, ideas for making connections to students' language and cultures, included on the Preview page, help the class explore the unit's concepts from a multicultural perspective.

Materials

A complete list of the materials needed for teaching this unit is found on p. I-15. Some of these materials are available in kits for the *Investigations* curriculum. Individual items can also be purchased from school supply dealers.

Classroom Materials In an active mathematics classroom, certain basic materials should be available at all times: interlocking cubes, pencils, unlined paper, graph paper, calculators, things to count with, and measuring tools. Some activities in this curriculum require scissors and glue sticks or tape. Stick-on notes and large paper are also useful materials throughout.

So that students can independently get what they need at any time, they should know where these materials are kept, how they are stored, and how they are to be returned to the storage area. For example, interlocking cubes are best stored in towers of ten; then, whatever the activity, they should be returned to storage in groups of ten at the end of the hour. You'll find that establishing such routines at the beginning of the year is well worth the time and effort.

Technology Calculators are used throughout *Investigations.* Many of the units recommend that you have at least one calculator for each pair. You will find calculator activities, plus Teacher Notes discussing this important mathematical tool, in an early unit at each grade level. It is assumed that calculators will be readily available for student use.

Computer activities at grade 3 use two software programs that were developed especially for the *Investigations* curriculum. *Tumbling Tetrominoes* is introduced in the 2-D Geometry unit, *Flips, Turns, and Area.* This game emphasizes ideas about area and about geometric motions (slides, flips, and turns). The program *Geo-Logo*™ is introduced in a second 2-D Geometry unit, *Turtle Paths,* where students use it to explore geometric shapes.

How you use the computer activities depends on the number of computers you have available. Suggestions are offered in the geometry units for how to organize different types of computer environments.

Children's Literature Each unit offers a list of suggested children's literature (p. I-15) that can be used to support the mathematical ideas in the unit. Sometimes an activity is based on a specific children's book, with suggestions for substitutions where practical. While such activities can be adapted and taught without the book, the literature offers a rich introduction and should be used whenever possible.

Student Sheets and Teaching Resources Student recording sheets and other teaching tools needed for both class and homework are provided as reproducible blackline masters at the end of each unit. They are also available as Student Activity Booklets. These booklets contain all the sheets each student will need for individual work, freeing you from extensive copying (although you may need or want to copy the occasional teaching resource on transparency film or card stock, or make extra copies of a student sheet).

We think it's important that students find their own ways of organizing and recording their work. They need to learn how to explain their thinking with both drawings and written words, and how to organize their results so someone else can

Name Date

Student Sheet 11

Make a Shape

Make a shape with an area of 5, 6, or 7 square units.
Draw it on the dot grid.
Use both squares and triangles in your shape.

What is the area of your shape? ______
Write how you know your shape has that area.

© Dale Seymour Publications® 72 *Investigation 2 • Sessions 4–5 Flips, Turns, and Area*

understand them. For this reason, we deliberately do not provide student sheets for every activity. Regardless of the form in which students do their work, we recommend that they keep a mathematics notebook or folder so that their work is always available for reference.

Homework In *Investigations,* homework is an extension of classroom work. Sometimes it offers review and practice of work done in class, sometimes preparation for upcoming activities, and sometimes numerical practice that revisits work in earlier units. Homework plays a role both in supporting students' learning and in helping inform families about the ways in which students in this curriculum work with mathematical ideas.

Depending on your school's homework policies and your own judgment, you may want to assign more homework than is suggested in the units. For this purpose you might use the practice pages, included as blackline masters at the end of this unit, to give students additional work with numbers.

For some homework assignments, you will want to adapt the activity to meet the needs of a variety of students in your class: those with special needs, those ready for more challenge, and second-language learners. You might change the numbers in a problem, make the activity more or less complex, or go through a sample activity with those who need extra help. You can modify any student sheet for either homework or class use. In particular, making numbers in a problem smaller or larger can make the same basic activity appropriate for a wider range of students.

Another issue to consider is how to handle the homework that students bring back to class—how to recognize the work they have done at home without spending too much time on it. Some teachers hold a short group discussion of different approaches to the assignment; others ask students to share and discuss their work with a neighbor, or post the homework around the room and give students time to tour it briefly. If you want to keep track of homework students bring in, be sure it ends up in a designated place.

***Investigations* at Home** It is a good idea to make your policy on homework explicit to both students and their families when you begin teaching with *Investigations*. How frequently will you be assigning homework? When do you expect homework to be completed and brought back to school? What are your goals in assigning homework? How independent should families expect their children to be? What should the parent's or guardian's role be? The more explicit you can be about your expectations, the better the homework experience will be for everyone.

Investigations at Home (a booklet available separately for each unit, to send home with students) gives you a way to communicate with families about the work students are doing in class. This booklet includes a brief description of every session, a list of the mathematics content emphasized in each investigation, and a discussion of each homework assignment to help families more effectively support their children. Whether or not you are using the *Investigations* at Home booklets, we expect you to make your own choices about homework assignments. Feel free to omit any and to add extra ones you think are appropriate.

Family Letter A letter that you can send home to students' families is included with the blackline masters for each unit. Families need to be informed about the mathematics work in your classroom; they should be encouraged to participate in and support their children's work. A reminder to send home the letter for each unit appears in one of the early investigations. These letters are also available separately in Spanish, Vietnamese, Cantonese, Hmong, and Cambodian.

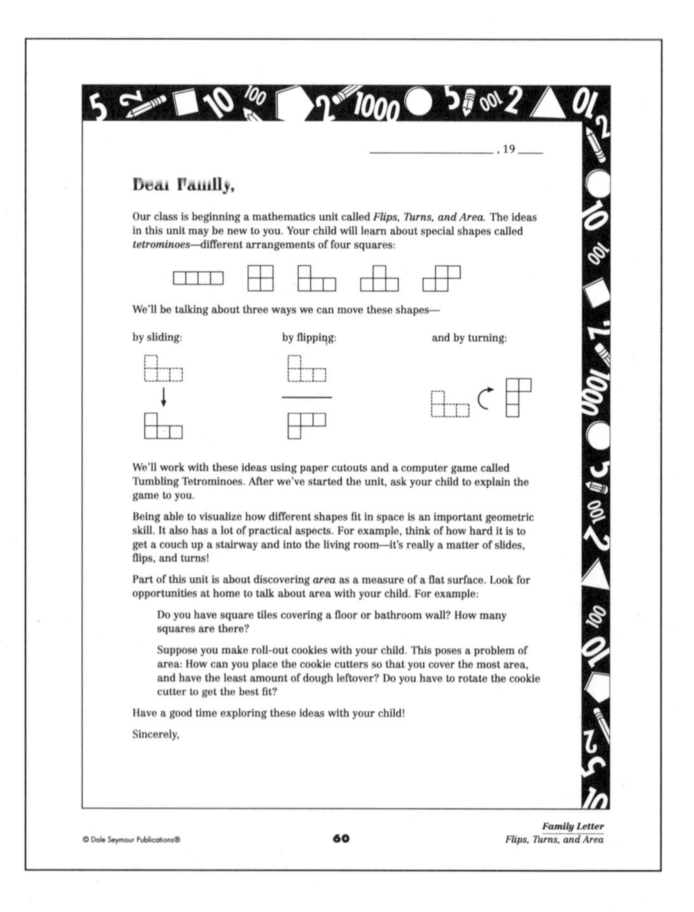

_______________, 19____

Dear Family,

Our class is beginning a mathematics unit called *Flips, Turns, and Area.* The ideas in this unit may be new to you. Your child will learn about special shapes called *tetrominoes*—different arrangements of four squares:

We'll be talking about three ways we can move these shapes—

by sliding: by flipping: and by turning:

We'll work with these ideas using paper cutouts and a computer game called Tumbling Tetrominoes. After we've started the unit, ask your child to explain the game to you.

Being able to visualize how different shapes fit in space is an important geometric skill. It also has a lot of practical aspects. For example, think of how hard it is to get a couch up a stairway and into the living room—it's really a matter of slides, flips, and turns!

Part of this unit is about discovering *area* as a measure of a flat surface. Look for opportunities at home to talk about area with your child. For example:

> Do you have square tiles covering a floor or bathroom wall? How many squares are there?
>
> Suppose you make roll-out cookies with your child. This poses a problem of area: How can you place the cookie cutters so that you cover the most area, and have the least amount of dough leftover? Do you have to rotate the cookie cutter to get the best fit?

Have a good time exploring these ideas with your child!

Sincerely,

 60 *Family Letter* *Flips, Turns, and Area*

Help for You, the Teacher

Because we believe strongly that a new curriculum must help teachers think in new ways about mathematics and about their students' mathematical thinking processes, we have included a great deal of material to help you learn more about both.

About the Mathematics in This Unit This introductory section (p. I-16) summarizes the critical information about the mathematics you will be teaching. It describes the unit's central mathematical ideas and how students will encounter them through the unit's activities.

Teacher Notes These reference notes provide practical information about the mathematics you are teaching and about our experience with how students learn. Many of the notes were written in response to actual questions from teachers, or to discuss important things we saw happening in the field-test classrooms. Some teachers like to read them all before starting the unit, then review them as they come up in particular investigations.

Dialogue Boxes Sample dialogues demonstrate how students typically express their mathematical ideas, what issues and confusions arise in their thinking, and how some teachers have guided class discussions.

These dialogues are based on the extensive classroom testing of this curriculum; many are word-for-word transcriptions of recorded class discussions. They are not always easy reading; sometimes it may take some effort to unravel what the students are trying to say. But this is the value of these dialogues; they offer good clues to how your students may develop and express their approaches and strategies, helping you prepare for your own class discussions.

Where to Start You may not have time to read everything the first time you use this unit. As a first-time user, you will likely focus on understanding the activities and working them out with your students. Read completely through each investigation before starting to present it. Also read those sections listed in the Contents under the heading Where to Start (p. vi).

Directions for Tumbling Tetrominoes — Teacher Note

In the computer game Tumbling Tetrominoes, students use the tetromino shapes to cover as many squares as possible on a 120-unit rectangular region. This game emphasizes ideas about area and geometric motions—slides, flips, and turns.

Starting Up the Game

To open the game, either click on the Tumbling Tetrominoes icon and choose Open from the File menu, or double-click on the Tumbling Tetrominoes icon. When the title screen appears, press **<return>**.

After a few seconds, the game screen will appear. Across the very top of the screen is the *menu bar;* for more information on this, see the **Teacher Note,** Using the Menus in Tumbling Tetrominoes (p. 20).

Just below the menu bar you will see a long window that we call the tool bar. These tools will be explained later; for now, turn your attention to the large game screen.

Playing the Game

The following game directions are summarized on Student Sheet 2, How to Play Tumbling Tetrominoes. You may want to give students their own copies, but also keep these two pages posted near each computer.

At the beginning of a game, you will see the empty outline of a 12-by-10 rectangle on the screen. Your goal is to cover the space inside this rectangle as completely as possible with tetrominoes.

You are given one tetromino at a time to place in the rectangle; the one ready to be placed is float-

Sessions 2 and 3: Slides, Flips, and Turns ▪ 17

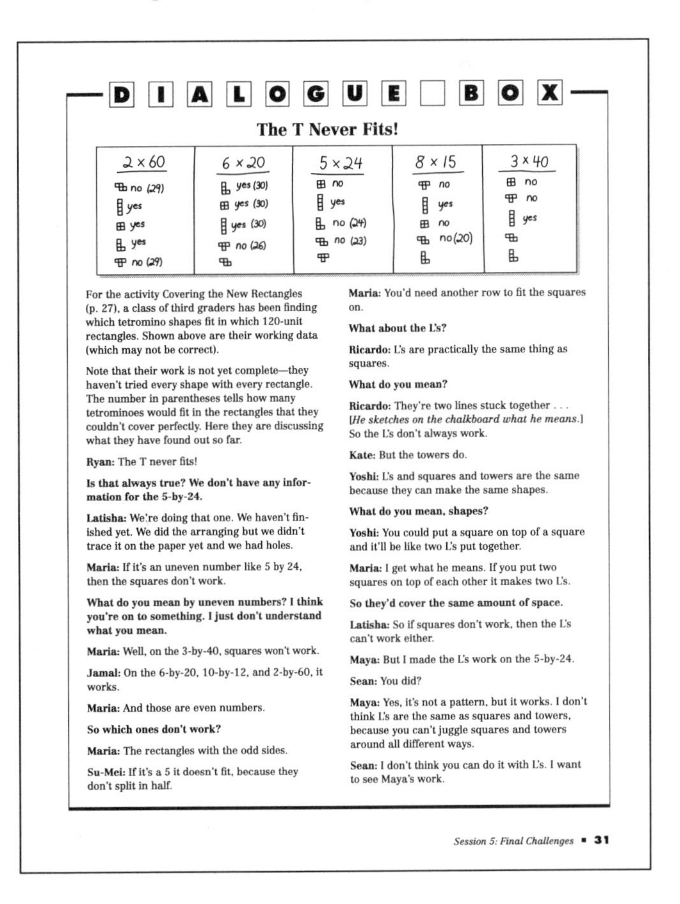

DIALOGUE BOX

The T Never Fits!

2 × 60	6 × 20	5 × 24	8 × 15	3 × 40
no (29)	yes (30)	no	no	no
yes	yes (30)	yes	yes	no
yes	yes (30)	no (24)	no	yes
yes	no (26)	no (23)	no(20)	
no (29)				

For the activity Covering the New Rectangles (p. 27), a class of third graders has been finding which tetromino shapes fit in which 120-unit rectangles. Shown above are their working data (which may not be correct).

Note that their work is not yet complete—they haven't tried every shape with every rectangle. The number in parentheses tells how many tetrominoes would fit in the rectangles that they couldn't cover perfectly. Here they are discussing what they have found out so far.

Ryan: The T never fits!

Is that always true? We don't have any information for the 5-by-24.

Latisha: We're doing that one. We haven't finished yet. We did the arranging but we didn't trace it on the paper yet and we had holes.

Maria: If it's an uneven number like 5 by 24, then the squares don't work.

What do you mean by uneven numbers? I think you're on to something. I just don't understand what you mean.

Maria: Well, on the 3-by-40, squares won't work.

Jamal: On the 6-by-20, 10-by-12, and 2-by-60, it works.

Maria: And those are even numbers.

So which ones don't work?

Maria: The rectangles with the odd sides.

Su-Mei: If it's a 5 it doesn't fit, because they don't split in half.

Maria: You'd need another row to fit the squares on.

What about the L's?

Ricardo: L's are practically the same thing as squares.

What do you mean?

Ricardo: They're two lines stuck together . . . [*He sketches on the chalkboard what he means.*] So the L's don't always work.

Kate: But the towers do.

Yoshi: L's and squares and towers are the same because they can make the same shapes.

What do you mean, shapes?

Yoshi: You could put a square on top of a square and it'll be like two L's put together.

Maria: I get what he means. If you put two squares on top of each other it makes two L's.

So they'd cover the same amount of space.

Latisha: So if squares don't work, then the L's can't work either.

Maya: But I made the L's work on the 5-by-24.

Sean: You did?

Maya: Yes, it's not a pattern, but it works. I don't think L's are the same as squares and towers, because you can't juggle squares and towers around all different ways.

Sean: I don't think you can do it with L's. I want to see Maya's work.

Session 5: Final Challenges ▪ 31

The *Investigations* curriculum incorporates the use of two forms of technology in the classroom: calculators and computers. Calculators are assumed to be standard classroom materials, available for student use in any unit. Computers are explicitly linked to one or more units at each grade level; they are used with the unit on 2-D geometry at each grade, as well as with some of the units on measuring, data, and changes.

Using Calculators

In this curriculum, calculators are considered tools for doing mathematics, similar to pattern blocks or interlocking cubes. Just as with other tools, students must learn both *how* to use calculators correctly and *when* they are appropriate to use. This knowledge is crucial for daily life, as calculators are now a standard way of handling numerical operations, both at work and at home.

Using a calculator correctly is not a simple task; it depends on a good knowledge of the four operations and of the number system, so that students can select suitable calculations and also determine what a reasonable result would be. These skills are the basis of any work with numbers, whether or not a calculator is involved.

Unfortunately, calculators are often seen as tools to check computations with, as if other methods are somehow more fallible. Students need to understand that any computational method can be used to check any other; it's just as easy to make a mistake on the calculator as it is to make a mistake on paper or with mental arithmetic. Throughout this curriculum, we encourage students to solve computation problems in more than one way in order to double-check their accuracy. We present mental arithmetic, paper-and-pencil computation, and calculators as three possible approaches.

In this curriculum we also recognize that, despite their importance, calculators are not always appropriate in mathematics instruction. Like any tools, calculators are useful for some tasks, but not for others. You will need to make decisions about when to allow students access to calculators and when to ask that they solve problems without them, so that they can concentrate on other tools and skills. At times when calculators are or are not appropriate for a particular activity, we make specific recommendations. Help your students develop their own sense of which problems they can tackle with their own reasoning and which ones might be better solved with a combination of their own reasoning and the calculator.

Managing calculators in your classroom so that they are a tool, and not a distraction, requires some planning. When calculators are first introduced, students often want to use them for everything, even problems that can be solved quite simply by other methods. However, once the novelty wears off, students are just as interested in developing their own strategies, especially when these strategies are emphasized and valued in the classroom. Over time, students will come to recognize the ease and value of solving problems mentally, with paper and pencil, or with manipulatives, while also understanding the power of the calculator to facilitate work with larger numbers.

Experience shows that if calculators are available only occasionally, students become excited and distracted when they are permitted to use them. They focus on the tool rather than on the mathematics. In order to learn when calculators are appropriate and when they are not, students must have easy access to them and use them routinely in their work.

If you have a calculator for each student, and if you think your students can accept the responsibility, you might allow them to keep their calculators with the rest of their individual materials, at least for the first few weeks of school. Alternatively, you might store them in boxes on a shelf, number each calculator, and assign a corresponding number to each student. This system can give students a sense of ownership while also helping you keep track of the calculators.

Using Computers

Students can use computers to approach and visualize mathematical situations in new ways. The computer allows students to construct and manipulate geometric shapes, see objects move according to rules they specify, and turn, flip, and repeat a pattern.

This curriculum calls for computers in units where they are a particularly effective tool for learning mathematics content. One unit on 2-D geometry at each of the grades 3–5 includes a core of activities that rely on access to computers, either in the classroom or in a lab. Other units on geometry, measurement, data, and changes include computer activities, but can be taught without them. In these units, however, students' experience is greatly enhanced by computer use.

The following list outlines the recommended use of computers in this curriculum:

Grade 1
Unit: *Survey Questions and Secret Rules* (Collecting and Sorting Data)
Software: Tabletop, Jr.
Source: Broderbund

Unit: *Quilt Squares and Block Towns* (2-D and 3-D Geometry)
Software: *Shapes*
Source: provided with the unit

Grade 2
Unit: *Mathematical Thinking at Grade 2* (Introduction)
Software: *Shapes*
Source: provided with the unit

Unit: *Shapes, Halves, and Symmetry* (Geometry and Fractions)
Software: *Shapes*
Source: provided with the unit

Unit: *How Long? How Far?* (Measuring)
Software: *Geo-Logo*
Source: provided with the unit

Grade 3
Unit: *Flips, Turns, and Area* (2-D Geometry)
Software: *Tumbling Tetrominoes*
Source: provided with the unit

Unit: *Turtle Paths* (2-D Geometry)
Software: *Geo-Logo*
Source: provided with the unit

Grade 4
Unit: *Sunken Ships and Grid Patterns* (2-D Geometry)
Software: *Geo-Logo*
Source: provided with the unit

Grade 5
Unit: *Picturing Polygons* (2-D Geometry)
Software: *Geo-Logo*
Source: provided with the unit

Unit: *Patterns of Change* (Tables and Graphs)
Software: *Trips*
Source: provided with the unit

Unit: *Data: Kids, Cats, and Ads* (Statistics)
Software: Tabletop, Sr.
Source: Broderbund

The software provided with the *Investigations* units uses the power of the computer to help students explore mathematical ideas and relationships that cannot be explored in the same way with physical materials. With the *Shapes* (grades 1–2) and *Tumbling Tetrominoes* (grade 3) software, students explore symmetry, pattern, rotation and reflection, area, and characteristics of 2-D shapes. With the *Geo-Logo* software (grades 3–5), students investigate rotations and reflections, coordinate geometry, the properties of 2-D shapes, and angles. The *Trips* software (grade 5) is a mathematical exploration of motion in which students run experiments and interpret data presented in graphs and tables.

We suggest that students work in pairs on the computer; this not only maximizes computer resources but also encourages students to consult, monitor, and teach one another. Generally, more than two students at one computer find it difficult to share. Managing access to computers is an issue for every classroom. The curriculum gives you explicit support for setting up a system. The units are structured on the assumption that you have enough computers for half your students to work on the machines in pairs at one time. If you do not have access to that many computers, suggestions are made for structuring class time to use the unit with five to eight computers, or even with fewer than five.

Assessment plays a critical role in teaching and learning, and it is an integral part of the *Investigations* curriculum. For a teacher using these units, assessment is an ongoing process. You observe students' discussions and explanations of their strategies on a daily basis and examine their work as it evolves. While students are busy recording and representing their work, working on projects, sharing with partners, and playing mathematical games, you have many opportunities to observe their mathematical thinking. What you learn through observation guides your decisions about how to proceed. In any of the units, you will repeatedly consider questions like these:

- Do students come up with their own strategies for solving problems, or do they expect others to tell them what to do? What do their strategies reveal about their mathematical understanding?
- Do students understand that there are different strategies for solving problems? Do they articulate their strategies and try to understand other students' strategies?
- How effectively do students use materials as tools to help with their mathematical work?
- Do students have effective ideas for keeping track of and recording their work? Does keeping track of and recording their work seem difficult for them?

You will need to develop a comfortable and efficient system for recording and keeping track of your observations. Some teachers keep a clipboard handy and jot notes on a class list or on adhesive labels that are later transferred to student files. Others keep loose-leaf notebooks with a page for each student and make weekly notes about what they have observed in class.

Assessment Tools in the Unit

With the activities in each unit, you will find questions to guide your thinking while observing the students at work. You will also find two built-in assessment tools: Teacher Checkpoints and embedded Assessment activities.

Teacher Checkpoints The designated Teacher Checkpoints in each unit offer a time to "check in" with individual students, watch them at work, and ask questions that illuminate how they are thinking.

At first it may be hard to know what to look for, hard to know what kinds of questions to ask. Students may be reluctant to talk; they may not be accustomed to having the teacher ask them about their work, or they may not know how to explain their thinking. Two important ingredients of this process are asking students open-ended questions about their work and showing genuine interest in how they are approaching the task. When students see that you are interested in their thinking and are counting on them to come up with their own ways of solving problems, they may surprise you with the depth of their understanding.

Teacher Checkpoints also give you the chance to pause in the teaching sequence and reflect on how your class is doing overall. Think about whether you need to adjust your pacing: Are most students fluent with strategies for solving a particular kind of problem? Are they just starting to formulate good strategies? Or are they still struggling with how to start? Depending on what you see as the students work, you may want to spend more time on similar problems, change some of the problems to use smaller numbers, move quickly to more challenging material, modify subsequent activities for some students, work on particular ideas with a small group, or pair students who have good strategies with those who are having more difficulty.

Embedded Assessment Activities Assessment activities embedded in each unit will help you examine specific pieces of student work, figure out what it means, and provide feedback. From the students' point of view, these assessment activities are no different from any others. Each is a learning experience in and of itself, as well as an opportunity for you to gather evidence about students' mathematical understanding.

The embedded assessment activities sometimes involve writing and reflecting; at other times, a discussion or brief interaction between student and teacher; and in still other instances, the creation and explanation of a product. In most cases, the assessments require that students *show* what they did, *write* or *talk* about it, or do both. Having to explain how they worked through a problem helps students be more focused and clear in their mathematical thinking. It also helps them realize that doing mathematics is a process that may involve tentative starts, revising one's approach, taking different paths, and working through ideas.

Teachers often find the hardest part of assessment to be interpreting their students' work. We provide guidelines to help with that interpretation. If you have used a process approach to teaching writing, the assessment in *Investigations* will seem familiar. For many of the assessment activities, a Teacher Note provides examples of student work and a commentary on what it indicates about student thinking.

Documentation of Student Growth

To form an overall picture of mathematical progress, it is important to document each student's work in journals, notebooks, or portfolios. The choice is largely a matter of personal preference; some teachers have students keep a notebook or folder for each unit, while others prefer one mathematics notebook, or a portfolio of selected work for the entire year. The final activity in each *Investigations* unit, called Choosing Student Work to Save, helps you and the students select representative samples for a record of their work.

This kind of regular documentation helps you synthesize information about each student as a mathematical learner. From different pieces of evidence, you can put together the big picture. This synthesis will be invaluable in thinking about where to go next with a particular child, deciding where more work is needed, or explaining to parents (or other teachers) how a child is doing.

If you use portfolios, you need to collect a good balance of work, yet avoid being swamped with an overwhelming amount of paper. Following are some tips for effective portfolios:

- Collect a representative sample of work, including some pieces that students themselves select for inclusion in the portfolio. There should be just a few pieces for each unit, showing different kinds of work—some assignments that involve writing, as well as some that do not.
- If students do not date their work, do so yourself so that you can reconstruct the order in which pieces were done.
- Include your reflections on the work. When you are looking back over the whole year, such comments are reminders of what seemed especially interesting about a particular piece; they can also be helpful to other teachers and to parents. Older students should be encouraged to write their own reflections about their work.

Assessment Overview

There are two places to turn for a preview of the assessment opportunities in each *Investigations* unit. The Assessment Resources column in the unit Overview Chart (pp. I-13–I-14) identifies the Teacher Checkpoints and Assessment activities embedded in each investigation, guidelines for observing the students that appear within classroom activities, and any Teacher Notes and Dialogue Boxes that explain what to look for and what types of student responses you might expect to see in your classroom. Additionally, the section About the Assessment in This Unit (p. I-17) gives you a detailed list of questions for each investigation, keyed to the mathematical emphases, to help you observe student growth.

Depending on your situation, you may want to provide additional assessment opportunities. Most of the investigations lend themselves to more frequent assessment, simply by having students do more writing and recording while they are working.

Flips, Turns, and Area

Content of This Unit Students explore shape and area through *tetrominoes*—arrangements of four squares with full sides touching. They variously use interlocking cubes, paper cutouts, and the computer as they try to cover rectangles with their tetrominoes. In the process, they investigate patterns, congruence, ideas about area, and the three geometric motions—slides, flips (reflections), and turns (rotations). In the second half of the unit, students explore area and congruence further, using square and triangle pieces to build shapes of a given area.

You can implement this unit with or without computers. There are suggestions for different ways to structure the unit, depending on how much computer access you have. The unit has been successfully used in classrooms with no computer access.

Connections with Other Units If you are doing the full-year *Investigations* curriculum in the suggested sequence for grade 3, this is the third of 10 units. Students will find connections between their work with area in this unit and their work with arrays in the previous unit, *Things That Come in Groups,* in which rectangular arrays are used to help students visualize multiplication and division relationships.

This unit can be used successfully at either grade 3 or grade 4, depending on the previous experience and needs of your students.

Investigations Curriculum ■ Suggested Grade 3 Sequence

Mathematical Thinking at Grade 3 (Introduction)

Things That Come in Groups (Multiplication and Division)

▶ *Flips, Turns, and Area* (2-D Geometry)

From Paces to Feet (Measuring and Data)

Landmarks in the Hundreds (The Number System)

Up and Down the Number Line (Changes)

Combining and Comparing (Addition and Subtraction)

Turtle Paths (2-D Geometry)

Fair Shares (Fractions)

Exploring Solids and Boxes (3-D Geometry)

Investigation 1 ▪ Motions with Tetrominoes

Class Sessions	Activities	Pacing
Session 1 (p. 4) TETROMINOES	Creating Different Shapes with Four Squares Covering a Rectangle with One Shape Homework: Making Tetrominoes Extension: 3-D Tetrominoes Extension: Floor Tetrominoes	minimum 1 hr
Sessions 2 and 3 (p. 10) SLIDES, FLIPS, AND TURNS	The Perfect Cover-Up Class Discussion: The Perfect Fit Tumbling Tetrominoes Tumbling Tetrominoes on Paper Teacher Checkpoint: Predicting Motions Class Discussion: Our Game Strategies Homework: The Perfect Cover-Up Homework: How Many Squares?	minimum 2 hr
Session 4 (p. 23) RECTANGLES WITH DIFFERENT SHAPES	Changing the Shape of the Rectangle Which Shapes Are Easiest to Cover? Homework: Making More Rectangles Extension: Possible Scores	minimum 1 hr
Session 5 (p. 27) FINAL CHALLENGES	Covering the New Rectangles Tumbling Tetrominoes: Star Level Assessment: Puzzle Pieces Extension: Extended Space-Covering Extension: Tetris™ Extension: Exploring Factors	minimum 1 hr

Ten-Minute Math ▪ Broken Calculator

Mathematical Emphasis

- Measuring area by covering a flat space with square units
- Finding systematically all possible geometric arrangements of a given number of squares
- Finding patterns for covering a space
- Comparing area of rectangles with different dimensions
- Describing physical motions in precise ways as a series of slides, flips, and turns
- Comparing two shapes to decide if they are congruent or not after using geometric motions—slides, flips, turns—to try fitting one shape exactly on top of the other

Assessment Resources

What's an -Omino? (Teacher Note, p. 8)

How Many Squares? (Dialogue Box, p. 9)

Teacher Checkpoint: Predicting Motions (p. 15)

Providing Appropriate Levels of Challenge (Teacher Note, p. 22)

Changing the Rectangle's Shape (Dialogue Box, p. 26)

Assessment: Puzzle Pieces (p. 28)

Tetrominoes on the 5-by-24 Rectangle (Dialogue Box, p. 30)

The T Never Fits! (Dialogue Box, p. 31)

Materials

Interlocking cubes

Resealable plastic bags or envelopes

Overhead projector, transparencies, and pens

Scissors, crayons, glue

Apple Macintosh disk Tumbling Tetrominoes

Computers—Macintosh II or above

Standard number cubes

Transparent or masking tape

Family letter

Student Sheets 1–6

Teaching resource sheet

Investigation 2 ▪ Finding Area

Class Sessions	Activities	Pacing
Session 1 (p. 34) TRIANGLES AND SQUARES	Solving the Tetromino Puzzle Measuring Flat Space Homework: What's My Score? Extension: Squares on the Floor Extension: Geoboards	minimum 1 hr
Sessions 2 and 3 (p. 39) A POSTER OF FOUR-UNIT SHAPES	Discussing Homework: Looking at Area Finding Shapes with an Area of Four Units Class Discussion: Creating New Shapes Class Discussion: Are These Two Shapes the Same? Homework: Squares! Squares! Squares! Homework: What's My Score? What's the Area? Extension: Tangrams	minimum 2 hr
Sessions 4 and 5 (p. 46) WRITING ABOUT AREA	Discussing Homework: Area at Home Finishing the Posters Assessment: Proving the Area of a Shape Choosing Student Work to Save Homework: More 4-Unit Shapes Extension: All Possible Shapes	minimum 2 hr

Ten-Minute Math ▪ Broken Calculator

Mathematical Emphasis

- Measuring area by covering a flat space with square units
- Comparing the area of two shapes by determining if they cover the same amount of flat space
- Comparing shapes to see if they are congruent through motions such as rotation (turns) and reflection (flips)
- Exploring relationships among shapes; for example, a rectangle can be cut into two triangles, each of which is half the area of the rectangle
- Finding the area of complex shapes by cutting them into recognizable smaller units of area such as square units and half units

Assessment Resources

Understanding the Area of Triangles (Teacher Note, p. 37)

The Space Is the Same (Dialogue Box, p. 38)

Assessment: Proving the Area of a Shape (p. 48)

Choosing Student Work to Save (p. 49)

Assessment: Proving the Area of a Shape (Teacher Note, p. 50)

The Area of My Shape is 5 (Dialogue Box, p. 52)

Materials

Overhead projector
Scissors, glue
Crayons or markers
Resealable plastic bags or envelopes
Large paper (11 × 17)
Tangram puzzles
Student Sheets 7–12
Teaching resource sheets

MATERIALS LIST

Following are the basic materials needed for the activities in this unit. Many of the items can be purchased from the publisher, either individually or in the Teacher Resource Package and the Student Materials Kit for grade 3. Detailed information is available on the *Investigations* order form. To obtain this form, call toll-free 1-800-872-1100 and ask for a Dale Seymour customer service representative.

Snap™ Cubes (interlocking cubes): 130 for each pair of students.

Resealable plastic bags, envelopes, or other containers for storing paper shapes: 1 per student

Computers (Macintosh II or above) with 4 MB of internal memory (RAM) and Apple System Software 7.0 or later: 1 per pair of students. (It is possible to modify the unit for fewer, or even no computers; see the **Teacher Note,** Managing the Computer Activities, p. 9.)

Apple Macintosh disk, Tumbling Tetrominoes, for *Flips, Turns, and Area* (packaged with this book)

A projection device attached to one computer for whole-class viewing (recommended)

Overhead projector, transparencies, and pens

Transparent or masking tape: available to each pair of students

Large paper for a poster (11-by-17-inch is an appropriate size): 1 per pair of students

Standard number cubes

Scissors, glue, crayons or markers

Tangram puzzles (optional)

Calculators (for Ten-Minute Math)

The following materials are provided at the end of this unit as blackline masters. A Student Activity Booklet containing all student sheets and teacher resources needed for individual work is available.

Family Letter (p. 60)

Student Sheets 1–12 (p. 61)

Teaching Resources:

  Square and Triangle Cutouts (p. 74)

  10-by-12 Rectangle (p. 75)

Practice Pages (p. 77)

Related Children's Literature

Tompert, Ann. *Grandfather Tang's Story.* New York: Crown Publishers, Inc. 1990.

Mathematics is more than the study of number. One of the other critical areas of mathematical work in the elementary grades is geometry. And geometry goes beyond the simple naming of shapes. In this unit, students study shapes in deeper ways: they move, divide, and combine shapes; they compare shapes to see if they are congruent; they measure their area. Such activities develop not only their geometric knowledge, but also their spatial visualization.

Students encounter three major ideas in this unit. The first idea is that you can measure area by choosing a square of a particular size to be your unit of area, and then finding the number of these square units that will cover a surface.

Students begin their study of area with rectangles and other shapes that can be covered easily with an array of squares. They later work with more complex shapes that they separate into recognizable smaller units of area—rectangles and triangles—in order to determine their area.

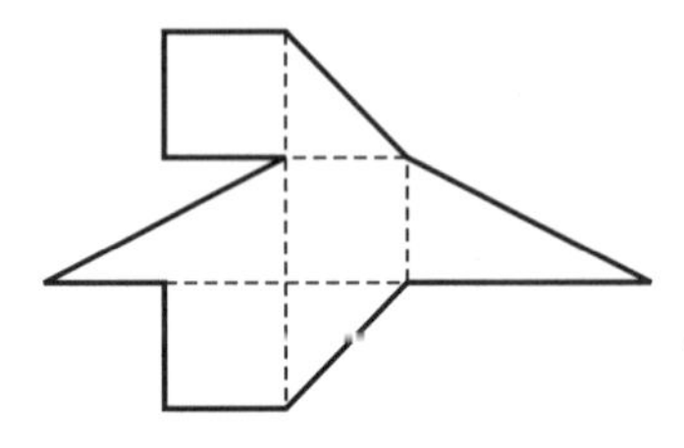

The area of a triangular shape can be figured out by seeing it in relation to a related rectangle. Visualizing a right triangle as half of a square or rectangle is an important tool in determining the area of many shapes.

The second focus of the unit is the idea of geometric motions. *Slides, flips* (reflections), and *turns* (rotations) account for all the ways we can move two-dimensional shapes. Students work with these motions as they fit shapes together to cover a particular area.

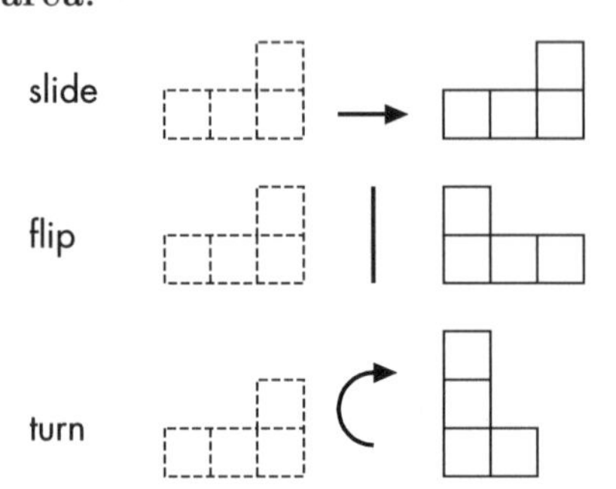

Students also use these motions as they explore the third major idea in this unit, the idea of *congruence*. Through comparison, you can determine whether two figures are the same size and same shape (that is, *congruent*). If they are congruent, there is a sequence of slides, flips, and turns that will move one exactly onto the other. Such movements will also enable you to compare the area of two different figures.

Students also encounter *connections* between shape and number. As they work to determine the area of a rectangle covered by square units, they might skip count by the number of squares in each row. Others might multiply the number in each row by the number of rows. Some might count one by one.

Students at this age should be encouraged to move beyond counting by 1's, inventing more efficient strategies for counting accurately. However, *do not teach them formulas for calculating area.* All too easily, students simply memorize these procedures without understanding what or why they are multiplying. First, students need to have many experiences in which they cover areas with square units; then they will develop strategies for counting these efficiently, which naturally lead to useful formulas in the later grades.

Mathematical Emphasis At the beginning of each investigation, the Mathematical Emphasis section tells you what is most important for students to learn about during that investigation. Many of these mathematical understandings and processes are difficult and complex. Students gradually learn more and more about each idea over many years of schooling. Students will begin and end the unit with different levels of knowledge and skill, but all will gain greater knowledge of area and shape and develop strategies for solving problems that involve these ideas.

Throughout the *Investigations* curriculum, there are many opportunities for ongoing daily assessment as you observe, listen to, and interact with students at work. In this unit, you will find one Teacher Checkpoint:

Investigation 1, Sessions 2–3
Predicting Motions (p. 15)

This unit also has two embedded assessment activities:

Investigation 1, Session 5
Puzzle Pieces (p. 28)

Investigation 2, Sessions 4–5
Proving the Area of a Shape (p. 48)

In addition, you can use almost any activity in this unit to assess your students' needs and strengths. Listed below are questions to help you focus your observation in each investigation. You may want to keep track of your observations for each student to help you plan your curriculum and monitor students' growth. Suggestions for documenting student growth can be found in the section About Assessment (p. I-10).

Investigation 1: Motions with Tetrominoes

- How do students relate the number of squares on a grid with how many cubes they will need to cover the grid? How do they figure out the total number of squares in the grid? the total number of cubes?
- What system or method do students use to find all the possible arrangements of four squares with full sides touching? Do they have a plan? Are they systematic in their approaches? Or do they try to find arrangements more randomly?
- How do students completely cover a 10-by-12 rectangle with cubes or paper tetrominoes? What strategies do they use to fit more shapes on a grid? Do they use patterns? Are they systematic in their approaches or more random?
- What strategies do students use to find the area of rectangles with different dimensions? How do they compare the area of rectangles with different dimensions?
- What language do students use to describe and discuss the motions used to fit tetrominoes onto a grid? Do students understand and use slides, turns, and flips as they work?
- How do students compare two shapes to decide if they are congruent or not? Do they compare them visually? Do they manipulate the shapes to compare them directly? Do they use flips, slides, and turns to check?

Investigation 2: Finding Area

- How do students determine the area of a flat space using square units? Do they use or consider relationships among shapes (for example, a triangle that is one-half a square unit)? How do they understand, explain, and prove that a square unit can be made of a non-square shape, such as a triangle? How do students explain their reasoning?
- How do students compare the area of two shapes? Do they count the number of pieces it takes to make a shape to figure out its area? Do they consider the amount of space inside? the number of units that will fit in that space? Do they recognize that the area is the same if the amount of flat space they cover is the same?
- How do students compare two shapes to decide if they are congruent or not? Do they compare them visually? Do they manipulate the shapes to compare them directly? Do they use reflections (flips) and rotations (turns) to check? Can they explain how or why two shapes are congruent without demonstrating it?
- How do students find and use relationships among shapes? What do they notice when comparing shapes of the same area that are made of different pieces? For example, how would they compare a square made of 4 squares with one made of 8 triangles?
- How do students find the area of complex shapes? Do they combine shapes that are not squares? Do they use smaller, more familiar units? How do students communicate their procedure for doing this? Do students understand how much area the half-unit and unit triangles cover?

PREVIEW FOR THE LINGUISTICALLY DIVERSE CLASSROOM

In the *Investigations* curriculum, mathematical vocabulary is introduced naturally during the activities. We don't ask students to learn definitions of new terms; rather, they come to understand such words as *factor* or *area* or *symmetry* by hearing them used frequently in discussion as they investigate new concepts. This approach is compatible with current theories of second-language acquisition, which emphasize the use of new vocabulary in meaningful contexts while students are actively involved with objects, pictures, and physical movement.

Listed below are some key words used in this unit that will not be new to most English speakers at this age level, but may be unfamiliar to students with limited English proficiency. You will want to spend additional time working on these words with your students who are learning English. If your students are working with a second-language teacher, you might enlist your colleague's aid in familiarizing students with these words, before and during this unit. In the classroom, look for opportunities for students to hear and use these words. Activities you can use to present the words are given in the appendix, Vocabulary Support for Second-Language Learners (p. 55).

copy, copies, L, T Students make and work with multiple *copies* of the tetromino shapes, including shapes commonly referred to as *L* and *T* shapes.

motion, slide, flip, turn Both in a computer game and working with shapes made of interlocking cubes or paper, students use three standard *motions—slides, flips,* and *turns*—as they fit the shapes together.

pieces, cover, fit In activities throughout the unit, students manipulate paper cutouts or *pieces* and shapes to *cover* rectangles of different shapes and sizes. They figure out how many squares will *fit* on another shape as a measure of the shape's area.

score In a computer game, students figure their *scores* by counting the number of squares they have covered.

possible, impossible Students must know these terms to explore questions like these: What are all *possible* shapes you can make with four squares? What is the highest score *possible* in this game? What scores are *impossible?*

Investigations

INVESTIGATION 1

Motions with Tetrominoes

What Happens

Session 1: Tetrominoes Students find all possible arrangements of four squares, called *tetrominoes*. They use informal language to describe the motions they can use to overlay two shapes for comparison, to convince someone that one shape is or is not the same as another. They use a single tetromino repeatedly to make a pattern that will cover a 10-by-12 grid of squares.

Sessions 2 and 3: Slides, Flips, and Turns Students continue to explore how they can cover an area with tetrominoes. In the computer game, Tumbling Tetrominoes, they practice the three basic geometric motions—slides, flips, and turns. There are two class discussions, one about the off-computer activity, one about the computer game; you will decide the best time to hold these, depending on when students have had enough experience with the activity to reflect on the discussion questions.

Session 4: Rectangles with Different Shapes Students construct different-shaped rectangles with the same area, cutting apart 10-by-12 grids and reassembling the pieces into new rectangles. Students also work on the computer game, Tumbling Tetrominoes, with different-shaped rectangles. They discuss the "fairness" of the different shapes, touching on ideas about conservation of area and strategies for covering.

Session 5: Final Challenges Students cover their different-shaped rectangles with tetrominoes and explore whether the same tetrominoes can cover these new rectangles as covered the original 10-by-12 grid. In the computer game, students are challenged to try the Star level, in which they cannot erase a move or flip the given shapes. As an assessment, students complete a puzzle that requires them to visualize the motions they've been using.

Mathematical Emphasis

- Measuring area by covering a flat space with square units
- Finding systematically all possible geometric arrangements of a given number of squares
- Finding patterns for covering a space
- Comparing areas of rectangles with different dimensions
- Describing physical motions in precise ways as a series of slides, flips, and turns
- Comparing two shapes to decide if they are congruent or not after using geometric motions—slides, flips, and turns—to try fitting one shape exactly on top of the other

What to Plan Ahead of Time

Materials

- Interlocking cubes: 130 per pair (Sessions 1–3)
- Resealable plastic bags or envelopes: 1 per student (Session 1)
- Overhead projector, transparencies and pens (Sessions 1–2)
- Scissors, crayons, glue (Sessions 2–3, 5)
- Apple Macintosh disk, Tumbling Tetrominoes, for *Flips, Turns, and Area* (Sessions 2–5)
- Computers (Macintosh II or above) with 4 MB of internal memory (RAM) and Apple System Software 7.0 or later: 1 per pair (Sessions 2–5)
- Standard number cubes and crayons or markers (Sessions 2–3, optional)
- Transparent or masking tape (Session 4)

Other Preparation

- If you plan to provide folders in which students will save their work for the entire unit, prepare these for distribution during Session 1.
- Try to make the set of tetrominoes yourself; see the **Teacher Note,** What's an –Omino? (p. 8) for directions. (Session 1)
- Use the disk for *Flips, Turns, and Area* to install the game Tumbling Tetrominoes on each available computer (see p. 57). Try the Tumbling Tetrominoes game. (Session 2)
- If you have fewer than the recommended computers, or none at all, see the **Teacher Note,** Managing the Computer Activities (p. 9), for alternative ways to present the unit. (Session 2)
- Prepare a 5-by-24 grid for each pair of students by cutting the 10-by-12 Rectangle (p. 75) in half lengthwise and taping the short ends together. (Session 5)
- Duplicate student sheets and teaching resources (located at the end of this unit) in the following quantities. If you have Student Activity Booklets, copy only the items marked with an asterisk, including any transparencies needed.

For all sessions

10-by-12 Rectangle (p. 75): at least 11 per student, and 1 transparency.* **Note:** This grid is used throughout the investigation for many purposes. The quantity needed will vary with your classroom and the choices you make; plan to make more copies as needed.

For Session 1

Student Sheet 1, Making Tetrominoes (p. 61): 1 per student (homework)

Family letter* (p. 60): 1 per student. Remember to sign it before copying.

For Sessions 2–3

Student Sheet 2, How to Play Tumbling Tetrominoes (p. 62): 1 per pair, or 1 per computer

Student Sheet 3, Game Records (p. 64): 1 per pair

Student Sheet 4, The Perfect Cover-Up (p. 65): 1 per student (homework)

Student Sheet 5, How Many Squares? (p. 66): 1 per student (homework)

For Session 5

Student Sheet 6, Puzzle Pieces (p. 67): 1 per student

Session 1

Tetrominoes

Materials

- Interlocking cubes (130 per pair)
- 10-by-12 Rectangle (1 per pair, 2 per student, homework)
- Transparency of 10-by-12 Rectangle
- Student Sheet 1 (1 per student, homework)
- Resealable plastic bags or envelopes (1 per student, homework)
- Family letter (1 per student)
- Overhead projector and pens

What Happens

Students find all possible arrangements of four squares, called *tetrominoes*. They use informal language to describe the motions they can use to overlay two shapes for comparison, to convince someone that one shape is or is not the same as another. They use a single tetromino repeatedly to make a pattern that will cover a 10-by-12 grid of squares. Their work focuses on:

- determining when two shapes are congruent
- describing how to move a shape in order to demonstrate its congruence to another shape
- finding a pattern to cover a rectangular space

Activity

Creating Different Shapes with Four Squares

Give each student or small groups of students interlocking cubes. Challenge students to generate all possible arrangements of four squares with full sides touching. If you are substituting square tiles for cubes, you may want to demonstrate on the overhead projector what "full sides touching" means. If you are using cubes, add the rule that they must lie flat—no stacking.

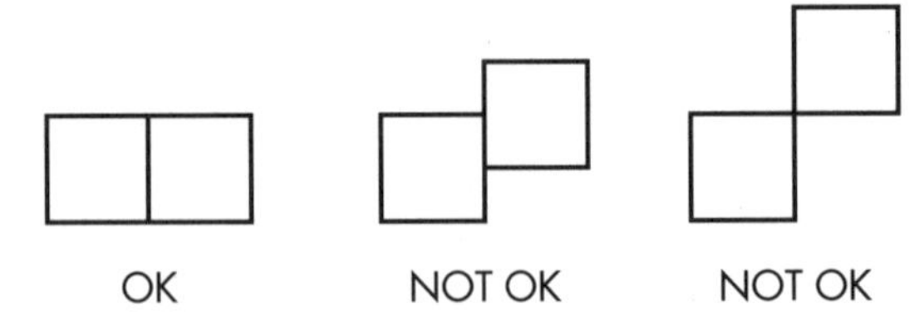

While students are working on this task, observe them and ask:

Could we give each shape a name? What do they look like to you?

Have the students invent names for the tetrominoes—such as "the L," "the T," and "the square"—and agree on what the whole class will call each one throughout the unit.

When student work has slowed down, start a whole-class discussion:

The shapes you have been making are all called *tetrominoes.* There are only a certain number of different tetromino shapes. Do you have them all? How do you know? Are some of these tetrominoes the same? Which ones? How could we prove it?

As students volunteer their ideas, encourage them to work at convincing others. They can use the overhead projector to demonstrate which shapes are the same, and how they know.

At this point, accept students' informal ideas and language as they discuss the motions they use on a tetromino to demonstrate that it is just like another; at the same time, you can use the terms *slide, flip,* and *turn* to describe their motions, as the students show what they are doing on the overhead projector.

You might also want to introduce *congruent* as the mathematical term for the idea "having exactly the same size and shape." That is, if one shape can be slid, flipped over, or turned to fit exactly on another shape, those two shapes are *congruent.* However, the emphasis in this session should not be on terminology, but on becoming familiar with the tetrominoes and ways of moving them.

Activity

Covering a Rectangle with One Shape

Hand out the 10-by-12 Rectangle, one copy to every pair of students, as you introduce the activity:

Pick your favorite tetromino, make a bunch of that shape with your cubes, and fit them together in a design that completely covers this rectangle. Try to fit as many of your particular tetromino shape as possible inside the rectangular frame, without any cubes hanging over or sticking out the sides of the rectangle. Also, remember to keep them flat—no cubes sticking up in a second layer.

As students work, ask them to think about these questions:

How many squares are there altogether on the grid?
How many squares did you cover with your tetromino design?
How did you figure out how many you covered?

See the **Dialogue Box,** How Many Squares? (p. 9), for a sample student discussion of these matters.

Note: Students will continue this same activity, with further discussion, in Session 2. You may want to collect the 10-by-12 Rectangles for later use.

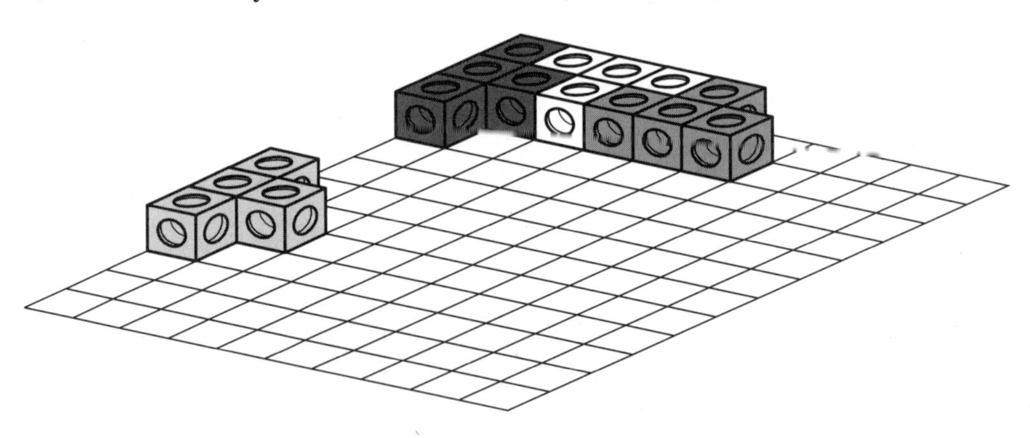

Session 1 Follow-Up

Homework

Making Tetrominoes Send home the family letter or *Investigations* at Home. Each student will also need Student Sheet 1, Making Tetrominoes, 2 copies of the 10-by-12 Rectangle, and a resealable plastic bag or envelope.

For homework, pick your favorite tetromino and make as many copies as you can from this grid paper. Color one tetromino at a time, then cut it out. Color and cut out as many as you can. You can throw away any left-over squares.

Make all four squares in each tetromino the same color. But if you want, each whole tetromino can be a different color. [*Demonstrate on the overhead with colored pens and the 10-by-12 Rectangle transparency.*]

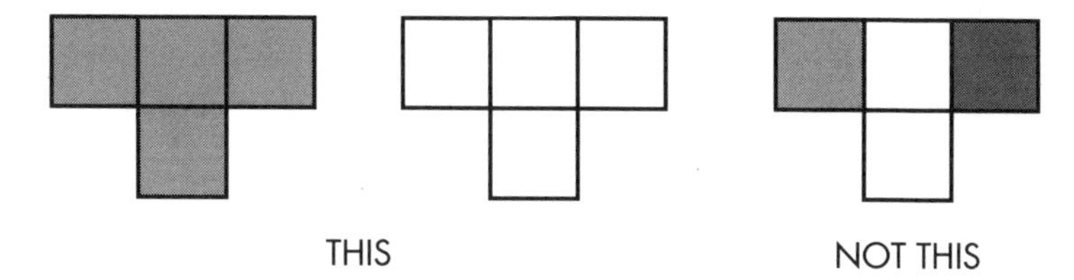

Count how many you made, and store them in your bag [or envelope]. Write down how many you have, and keep this number with your tetrominoes.

❖ **Tip for the Linguistically Diverse Classroom** As you give the instructions, model what is expected. Show a copy of Student Sheet 1 with one of the tetrominoes drawn many times. Demonstrate coloring one tetromino and cutting it out. To demonstrate that students can switch colors, but not within a single shape, pick another crayon and color half of a second tetromino. Pause and pick a third color, as if you are going to use it on the other half, but then stop, shaking your head. Put the third color back and hold up the same crayon you started coloring this shape with, nod happily, and finish coloring the tetromino.

Advise students that if they don't have scissors at home, they can do just the coloring; they can complete the cutting the next day in school.

Note: Students will continue working on this activity during the next two class sessions.

Extensions

3-D Tetrominoes Suggest that students explore the set of three-dimensional tetrominoes—all the shapes that can be made with four cubes, but *without* the constraint that they must lie flat. How many of these can they find?

Solution: There are three additional tetrominoes when 3-D shapes are allowed.

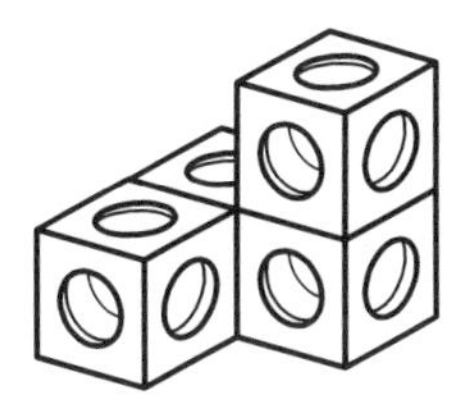

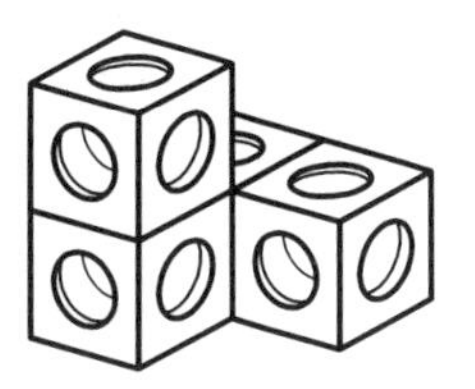

Floor Tetrominoes In one classroom with a checkerboard square pattern on the floor, students chalked tetrominoes on the floor and built large paper tetrominoes to fit over the squares, even covering a 10-by-12 rectangle with them. This extension is especially good for a class that enjoys large-motor activities.

Teacher Note   *What's an -Omino?*

A *domino,* as you may know, is the shape formed by putting two squares together, with full edges touching. There is only one shape you can make with two squares:

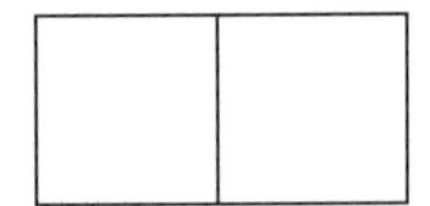

Adding a third square makes a *triomino.* A triomino has two possible arrangements:

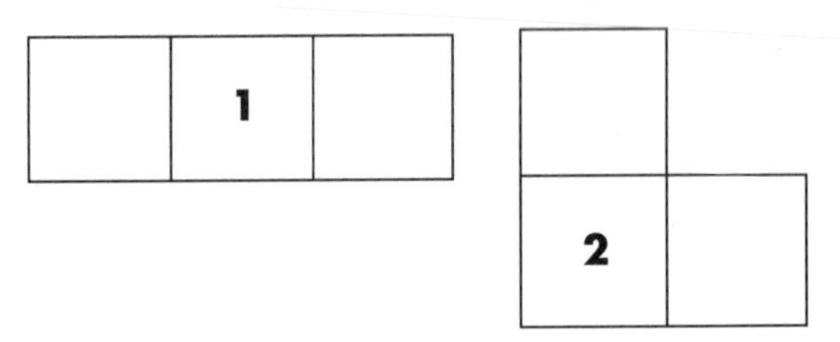

Triominoes A, B, and C may look like other possible arrangements, but they are actually the same shape as Triominoes 1 or 2.

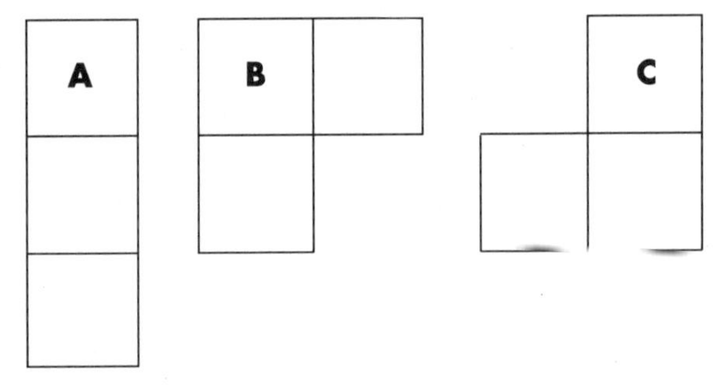

That is, we can move these shapes through space, with a *flip* (reflection) or a *turn* (rotation), and then a slide, to exactly match Triomino 1 or Triomino 2.

To see firsthand how this works, make Triomino B out of interlocking cubes or cut it from grid paper. Watch how you move it to make it look exactly like Triomino 2. Is there more than one series of motions that will work? Triomino 2 and Triomino B are congruent—the same size and shape. What about the other triominoes?

You should have discovered that Triomino B becomes Triomino 2 with a flip and a slide. Triomino A becomes Triomino 1 with a turn and a slide. And Triomino C becomes Triomino 2 with a 90-degree turn and a slide.

Now try making the set of *tetrominoes*—all the possible arrangements of *four* squares with full sides touching. Remember, if you can move a tetromino through a series of slides, flips, and turns so that it exactly matches another tetromino, it is not a different arrangement. When you think you have all the possible tetrominoes, compare yours with the pictures on Student Sheet 1, Making Tetrominoes (p. 61). Can you convince yourself that there cannot possibly be any other tetrominoes?

How Many Squares?

After students have spent some time trying to cover the 10-by-12 Rectangle with cube tetrominoes, they invent a variety of strategies for determining the total number of squares in the rectangle and the number of squares they have covered, as demonstrated in the following discussion.

How did you figure out the number of squares there are in the rectangle?

Sean: There's 118 squares. I counted every one.

Midori: No, it's 120. I took two towers of 5 on the bottom, and that was 10. There were 10 tens; 100. Then I counted by twos for the leftover columns and got 20. Then 100 and 20 is 120.

Tamara: I just counted by 10's: 10, 20, 30, 40, 50, 60, 70, 80, 90, 100, 110, 120.

Samir: I did it quicker by multiplying. See, there's 10 in every row. So, you just see that there's 12 of those, $10 \times 12 = 120$.

How did you figure out how many of those squares you covered?

Sean: I just counted all the squares. I covered 116.

Tamara: I knew there were 120 in all. So, I did it mathematically. I left 8 holes, so 120 take away 8 was . . . 112.

Samir: There's another way. I counted the number of tetrominoes I used to cover the rectangle. I used the "I" tetromino and it took 30 of them to cover the whole rectangle. Each tetromino is made of 4 little squares, so 30×4 is 120. See? I covered the whole rectangle!

Managing the Computer Activities

Teacher Note

The availability of computers to your students will determine how you organize the work in Sessions 2 through 5. Regardless of the number of computers available, have students work in pairs. This not only maximizes computer resources, but also encourages students to consult, monitor, and teach one another.

Computer Lab If you have a computer laboratory with one Apple Macintosh computer for each pair of students, you can conduct the activities in sequence. That is, you would begin Session 2 in class with the activity The Perfect Cover-Up, then move to the computer laboratory for Tumbling Tetrominoes.

Fewer Computers If you have fewer computers—from one to six in your classroom—you might want to use a choices or stations approach. To start Session 2 you would introduce both the off-computer activity, The Perfect Cover-Up, and the computer game, Tumbling Tetrominoes, to the whole class. Then, throughout Sessions 2 through 5, pairs of students would cycle through the computer game while the others work on the off-computer activities. Cycling pairs through the computer game throughout the school day, instead of just during your math hour, may be necessary to give everyone a chance at the computer within a reasonable number of days. Each pair should spend at least 20 minutes at the computer.

No Computers If you do not have a computer, you can use the activity Tumbling Tetrominoes on Paper (p. 14) as an alternative to the computer version.

Computer Help It helps to have reminders about particular keys and commands posted near the equipment. Establish rules for getting help from peers; one rule is to ask two other students before asking the teacher. Or, you might designate certain students as class computer consultants.

Sessions 2 and 3

Slides, Flips, and Turns

Materials

- Interlocking cubes (130 per pair)
- Students' envelopes of tetrominoes
- 10-by-12 Rectangle (1–6 per student)
- Scissors, crayons, glue (optional)
- Computers with Tumbling Tetrominoes installed
- Student Sheet 2 (1 per computer)
- Student Sheet 3 (1 per pair)
- Student Sheet 4 (1 per student, homework)
- Student Sheet 5 (1 per student, homework)

For the paper version of Tumbling Tetrominoes:

- 10-by-12 Rectangle (1 per student)
- One standard number cube
- Crayons or markers

What Happens

Students continue to explore how they can cover an area with tetrominoes. In the computer game, Tumbling Tetrominoes, they practice the three basic geometric motions—slides, flips, and turns. There are two class discussions, one about the off-computer activity, one about the computer game; you will decide the best time to hold these, depending on when students have had enough experience with the activity to reflect on the discussion questions. Their work focuses on:

- covering a rectangular region with tetrominoes of a single shape, looking for patterns and larger units
- forming conjectures as to why certain tetrominoes will cover the region completely and some will not
- giving explicit commands—slides, flips, and turns—to the computer to move tetrominoes to completely cover a rectangular region
- visualizing how one shape can be moved to best fit into a spatial arrangement of shapes

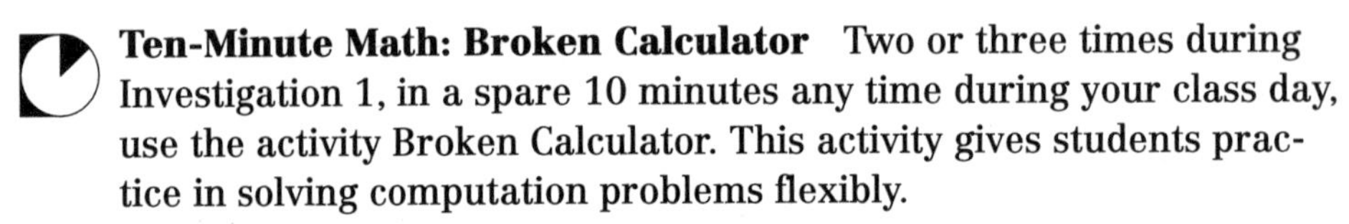

Ten-Minute Math: Broken Calculator Two or three times during Investigation 1, in a spare 10 minutes any time during your class day, use the activity Broken Calculator. This activity gives students practice in solving computation problems flexibly.

Pose problems like these:

Put 125 on your calculator screen without pressing 1 or 5.

Add 62 and 30 without pressing 3.

Add 48 and 48 without pressing 4 or 8.

After students solve the problem, list some of their solutions on the board. Ask students to choose one solution and extend it into a series that follows a pattern. For example, to form 125 without pressing 1 or 5:

$99 + 24 + 2 = 125$
$98 + 24 + 3 = 125$
$97 + 24 + 4 = 125$

For full directions and variations, see p. 53.

Activity

The Perfect Cover-Up

Distribute a copy of the 10-by-12 Rectangle to each student. They will be covering this grid with cubes as they did in Session 1, or with the paper tetrominoes they have been making. If students who want to use paper tetrominoes have not made at least 30 of the same shape, make available additional copies of the grid so they can continue coloring and cutting out tetrominoes, as they did for the Session 1 homework.

Today, you're going to try to cover a rectangle again, either with cubes or your paper tetrominoes. You can use only one shape, but as many copies of it as you need. You can slide, turn, or flip the shapes to get the best fit.

Students should find the best arrangement they can, covering as much of the rectangle as they can. Those who are using interlocking cubes can record their patterns by coloring in the squares to match the placement of the cube tetrominoes. Students using the paper cutouts can either paste them in place on the grid or color in their placement.

As you watch students work, make sure they know they can turn their shapes or flip them over. Ask questions like these:

Can you make a perfect fit? Are there many different ways to get a perfect fit? Are there strategies to get more of them to fit on the grid?

If you get a perfect fit with one shape, try to cover the rectangle with another tetromino. Which tetrominoes cover the whole rectangle perfectly?

As students work, ask questions to encourage them to recognize, expand, and reflect on their strategies:

I see you're using a pattern. Will it lead to a perfect fit if you continue to use that pattern?

Activity

Class Discussion: The Perfect Fit

This whole-class discussion will likely take place in Session 3, after all students have tried to cover the rectangle with several different tetrominoes. Ask them to share what they found out.

Which tetromino can you use to make a perfect fit? What strategy did you use to cover the rectangle? Did you use a pattern? Did you build another larger shape out of your tetromino? Which tetrominoes would not cover the rectangle? Why? Can you convince us there is no way the rectangle can be covered with that tetromino?

❖ **Tip for the Linguistically Diverse Classroom** In a discussion of this type, encourage all students to demonstrate as they share their ideas. For those who cannot yet verbalize responses, ask them to demonstrate their ideas as you narrate their actions.

The overhead projector would be useful for demonstrating students' strategies on the transparency of the 10-by-12 Rectangle. You may find that students used some of the following strategies:

- **Guess and Check** One beginning strategy is simply to place tetrominoes where they "look like" they fit, then change the placement if large holes appear. As they engage in both the off-computer and on-computer activities in these sessions, many students move beyond this and start thinking ahead, planning where each tetromino should go.
- **Patterns** Some students see that putting one tetromino "this way," then the next one "that way," in a pattern, leads to a perfect cover-up.

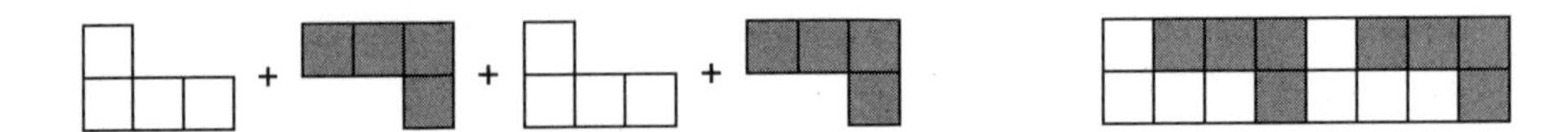

A Larger Unit An extension of patterning, this strategy is used by students who see that a certain number of tetrominoes can be put together to build a bigger unit, often one that is easy to use for covering.

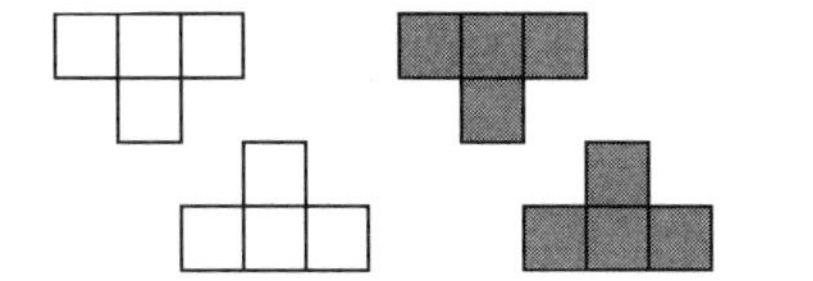

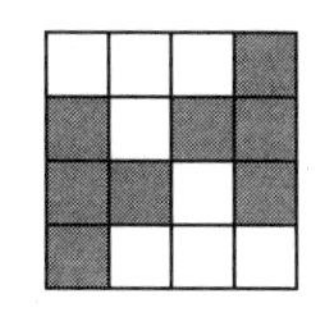

In this class discussion, you might hear comments like these:

Jeremy: L's and squares and towers are pretty much the same because they can make the same shapes.

What do you mean, shapes?

Jeremy: You could put a square on top of a square and it'll be like two L's put together.

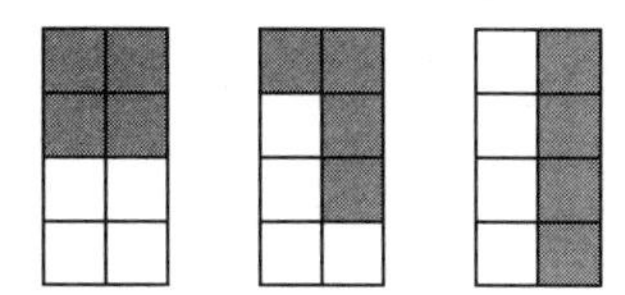

Ly Dinh: I get it. If you put two squares on top of each other, they make two L's.

Jeremy: Or two towers.

Activity

Tumbling Tetrominoes

Introduce the computer game to the whole class with a computer, a projection device for screen display (if available), and Student Sheet 2, How to Play Tumbling Tetrominoes. If you do not have a projection device, introduce the game at the computer to one small group at a time. You might want to develop "experts" who can teach the game to other students. For an explanation of the basic game and its options, see the **Teacher Note,** Directions for Tumbling Tetrominoes (p. 17).

Explain that the goal of the game is to place tetrominoes in a way that will cover the rectangle with as many squares as possible. The number of squares covered at the end of the game gives the players their score.

For their first games, students should be working with the 12-by-10 rectangle, which is automatically displayed when you open the game. They will be trying to cover rectangles with other dimensions in Session 4.

At the end of each game, students should record their scores on a copy of Student Sheet 3, Game Records. They should also save their work on the computer when their time is up, especially if they are in the middle of a game or want to replay their last game to check their strategies. They should also save their Game Records for continued use in the following several sessions.

Activity

Tumbling Tetrominoes on Paper

If you have few or no computers, students can play Tumbling Tetrominoes on paper. Each player is given a 10-by-12 Rectangle as a gameboard. The 10-unit edge is the bottom.

Make a key for numbers 1 through 6; each of the numbers 1–5 stands for a particular tetromino; 6 is Player's Choice. One, two, three, or four students can play together, each with a gameboard and colored markers or crayons.

One of the players rolls a number cube (players can take turns doing this). Then each player colors on his or her own gameboard the tetromino represented by that number. Players must "place" each tetromino with one side touching either the bottom or another already-placed tetromino, just as in the computer game. Play continues until no more tetrominoes can be placed. A player's total score is the number of squares covered.

In some classrooms, students have built the tetrominoes with interlocking cubes or have used cutout paper tetrominoes to place on their gameboards. Some teachers have made large number cubes with pictures of the tetrominoes on the faces. Even in classrooms with good computer access, many students enjoyed this off-computer version of Tumbling Tetrominoes.

Activity

Teacher Checkpoint

Predicting Motions

As students are working on the Tumbling Tetrominoes game, either on or off the computer, observe and interact with them individually.

See the next shape you have? Where are you going to put it? Why? What motions are you going to use to get it into place?

Observe to what degree students are using visualization abilities as they place the tetrominoes. See if and how they plan ahead. At first, it is fine for students to use trial and error as they become familiar with the shapes. However, as they get used to the game, encourage them to visualize where the piece will fit and how they will need to move it before they get it all the way down to where they are going to place it.

If students are playing in pairs, they can take turns directing each other how to move the tetromino. If some students are finding the game too easy, have them play at a more difficult level (see the **Teacher Note,** Providing Appropriate Levels of Challenge, p. 22).

Activity

Class Discussion: Our Game Strategies

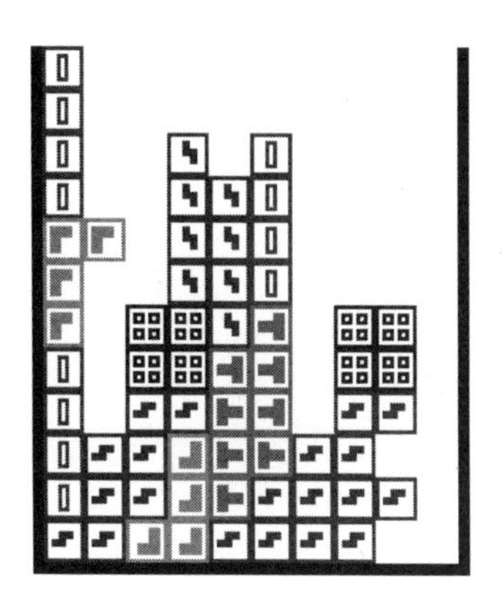

When all students have played Tumbling Tetrominoes at least once, gather the whole class for a discussion of the strategies they have discovered. Alternatively, you may want to have this discussion with small groups gathered around a computer.

Do certain shapes fit together well? How did you decide where to place the tetrominoes?

During this discussion, if you have a projection device or if you are working with small groups, you might use the Step tool to show one or more students' games, step by step, on the screen, as they describe their strategies.

Ask students about strategies they might use to avoid certain problematic situations. For example, in the situation shown at right, the player hasn't left enough room to slide an L tetromino into the gap at the lower right. Likewise, either an L or T would have fit in gaps on the lower left, but they can't slide down the narrow corridor. Use the Step tool on the computer to show these types of situations and discuss good moves, and to demonstrate why planning ahead is important.

Also ask students how they go about determining their score for a game.

How do you figure out how many squares you fit into the rectangle? What is the maximum score, the score of a perfect game?

Students might suggest either counting the covered space or subtracting the uncovered spaces from the maximum.

Sessions 2 and 3 Follow-Up

The Perfect Cover-Up Students continue working on The Perfect Cover-Up activity (p. 11), using Student Sheet 4, The Perfect Cover-Up, and additional copies of the 10-by-12 Rectangle for a base and for making more paper tetrominoes of a different shape.

Try to cover the rectangle again for homework. Remember, you can use only one shape, but use as many copies of it as you like. See if you can find a way to cover even more squares on your rectangle. Figure out the best arrangement you can, then paste or color in the tetrominoes on the grid. I'm giving you two pieces of grid paper, in case you want to cut out more tetrominoes.

Note: As an alternative to using the paper cutouts, students can simply color in the tetromino shapes on the grid, although this allows them less flexibility as they arrange them.

How Many Squares? After session 3, give each student a copy of Student Sheet 5, How Many Squares? Have students read the directions and discuss the task to make sure it is understood. This activity offers a good review of skip counting by 4's. You might also send home two 10-by-12 grids in case students actually need to cut and count the number of squares in the tetrominoes.

❖ **Tip for the Linguistically Diverse Classroom** For the last part of Student Sheet 4, allow students to write their explanations in their native languages or to convey their ideas entirely with diagrams and numerals.

Directions for Tumbling Tetrominoes

In the computer game Tumbling Tetrominoes, students use the tetromino shapes to cover as many squares as possible on a 120-unit rectangular region. This game emphasizes ideas about area and geometric motions—slides, flips, and turns.

Starting Up the Game

To open the game, either click on the Tumbling Tetrominoes icon and choose Open from the File menu, or double-click on the Tumbling Tetrominoes icon. When the title screen appears, press **<return>**.

After a few seconds, the game screen will appear. Across the very top of the screen is the *menu bar;* for more information on this, see the **Teacher Note,** Using the Menus in Tumbling Tetrominoes (p. 20).

Just below the menu bar you will see a long window that we call the tool bar. These tools will be explained later; for now, turn your attention to the large game screen.

Playing the Game

The following game directions are summarized on Student Sheet 2, How to Play Tumbling Tetrominoes. You may want to give students their own copies, but also keep these two pages posted near each computer.

At the beginning of a game, you will see the empty outline of a 12-by-10 rectangle on the screen. Your goal is to cover the space inside this rectangle as completely as possible with tetrominoes.

You are given one tetromino at a time to place in the rectangle; the one ready to be placed is float-

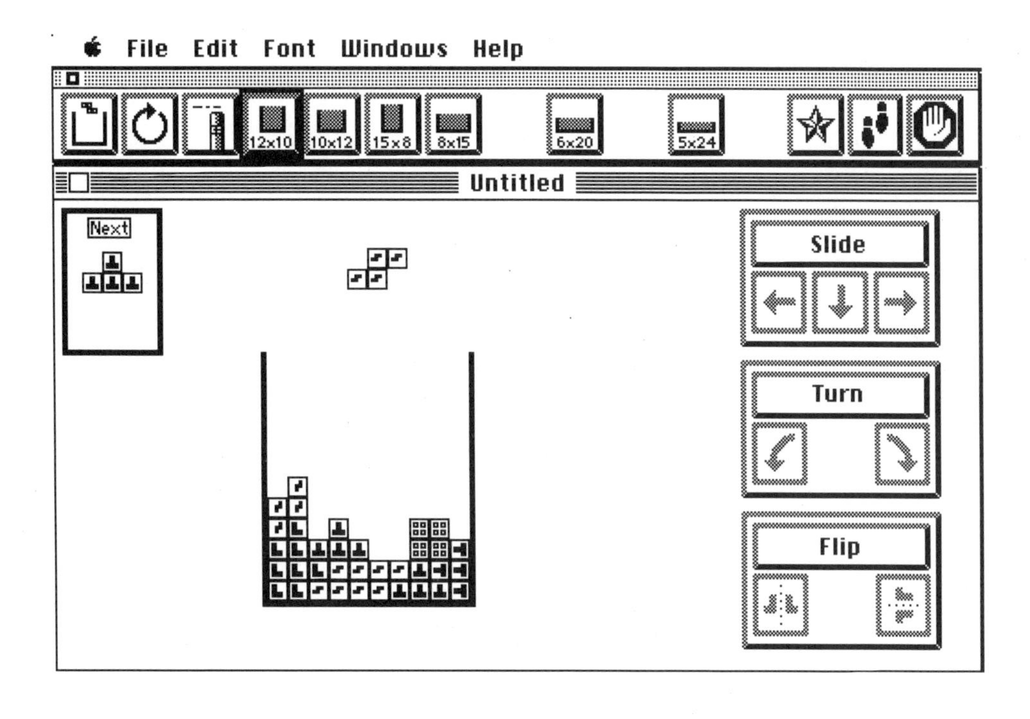

Teacher Note
continued

ing above the rectangular outline. The "Next" box (top left) shows you the next tetromino that will appear, enabling you to plan your moves. After you place each tetromino, the next one will appear in the "ready" position.

You can place a tetromino in the rectangle with any combination of three motions—Slide, Turn, and Flip. The direction buttons below each motion are dimmed (not available) until you have selected a motion. So, first select a motion by clicking on the Slide, Turn, or Flip button. When you do this, the buttons for that motion are then available (no longer dimmed). Choose the direction of the motion by clicking on one of these buttons. The best way to figure out these motions and how they work with the different tetrominoes is to experiment with them on the screen.

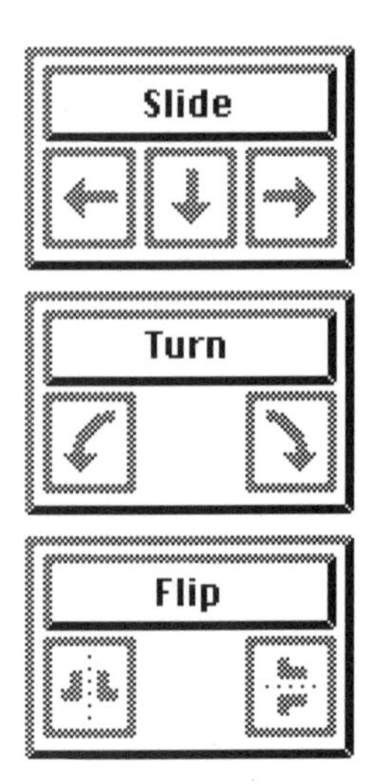

If you have students who have trouble using the mouse for any reason or who prefer to use keystrokes, there are keyboard alternatives for these basic moves. You can select Slide, Turn, or Flip by pressing the first letter of the motion (S, T, or F). Then use the arrow keys on the keyboard to complete the move.

When the bottom of the moving tetromino touches either the rectangle's base or another tetromino, it will stick there. If you want to slide it left or right after it has touched bottom, you must select the slide motion very quickly.

If you are sure about your placement and want to "drop" the tetromino quickly into position, clicking on Slide and pressing the spacebar once drops the tetromino directly down until it sticks.

If the tetromino fits entirely inside the rectangle—that is, if it doesn't poke out of the top border—it is stuck permanently. If the tetromino does *not* fit completely inside the rectangle—that is, if some of it pokes above the top border—the tetromino disappears.

When a tetromino sticks, the next one to be placed appears above the rectangle—moving over from the "Next" box.

The game is over when any one of three things happens:

1. Three tetrominoes have poked out of the top border and disappeared.
2. The rectangle is completely covered.
3. You click on the Stop tool.

Your final score is the number of unit squares you covered in the rectangle. Students figure out their scores and record them, for each game, on Student Sheet 3, Game Records.

If you must stop before you have completed a game—or if you finish a game that you want to share with the class for some reason—you may save your work and come back to it at some later time. For more information on saving a game, starting new games, and quitting, see the **Teacher Note,** Using the Menus in Tumbling Tetrominoes (p. 20).

Options

The following options appear in the tool bar at the top of the game screen. Student Sheet 2 (p. 62) provides a simple key to the tool bar.

Erase One

At any time, you can erase the placement of the last tetromino by clicking on the Erase One tool. If you repeatedly choose Erase One, you can keep erasing previous moves, one at a time. Introduce the Erase One tool to students as they show a need for it—that is, during a game when they first say they wish they had placed a tetromino differently.

Replay

Click on the Replay tool in the tool bar to replay the last game, choosing new moves if you like. The same tetrominoes will be presented in the same order, from the beginning. This gives you or someone else the chance to reflect on your strategies and try different ones.

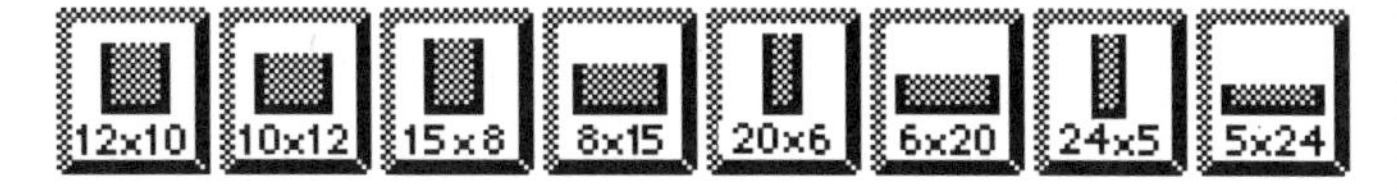

Rectangles

You can choose to cover a rectangle of a different shape by clicking on one of these rectangle icons. The area for each remains 120 units. This encourages discussion of the ease of covering different shapes, conservation of area, and how strategies might differ for different-shaped rectangles.

Note: Whether you have six or eight choices for rectangle shapes will depend on the size of your computer screen. All eight are shown if you have a 13-inch screen. If you have a 9-inch screen, six are shown; the two that would not fit on the screen do not appear on the tool bar.

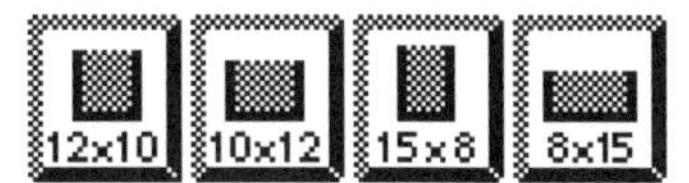

Star

If you click on the Star tool, you can play a game at a more challenging level. At the Star level you are not allowed to erase the placement of the last tetromino, nor can you do flips.

Step

If you click on the Step tool, each move in your last game will be shown exactly, step by step, with each click of the mouse. This is useful for demonstrations and discussions of strategies.

My Rectangle

An option called "My Rectangle" is purposely hidden so it does not confuse first-time players. Press option-M on the keyboard, and a new tool will appear next to the different-shaped rectangle icons in the tool bar—empty, with two question marks for its dimensions.

With this advanced option, you can choose a rectangle with any dimensions that will fit on your screen. When you click on this tool, you get a box asking you to choose the dimensions (in unit squares).

The dimensions available to you will vary with the size of your screen. For example, for a 9-inch screen, the height can be from 2 to 12; the width from 2 to 18. If you select a number outside the boundaries available to you, a box comes on the screen to state the limits.

Use the My Rectangle tool to create different and more challenging games. See the **Teacher Note,** Providing Appropriate Levels of Challenge (p. 22).

Scoring

Another option that is purposely hidden is automatic scoring. In general, students should figure out their own score (the area they covered, measured in number of squares) and record it on their copy of the Game Records (Student Sheet 3).

While we prefer to have students figure out their scores by themselves, you can press option-S to turn the scoring option on and off (it is initially off). When the scoring option is on, the score shows on the screen whenever a game ends.

In order to determine whether the scoring option is on or off before students begin the game, simply press option-S, and a box will appear to tell you.

Teacher Note — Using the Menus in Tumbling Tetrominoes

When you have opened a game of Tumbling Tetrominoes, the words you see across the top of the screen are called the *menu bar*. The most important menus for players of Tumbling Tetrominoes are the **File** menu and the **Help** menu. Students who are encouraged to use the computer for writing about their work will also be interested in the **Windows, Font,** and **Style** menus.

To see the items in a menu, point to the menu with the on-screen arrow and press the mouse button. Holding the mouse button down, drag the selection bar to different items on the menu. Release the button to select an item when it is highlighted.

The File Menu

The **File** menu may be used before you start playing—for example, to retrieve a previously saved game. Or, it may be used at the end of play when you are ready to print or save.

File

New Game	⌘N
Open My Game...	⌘O
Close My Game	⌘W
Save My Game	⌘S
Save My Game As...	
Page Setup...	
Print...	⌘P
Quit	⌘Q

New Game starts a new game. Of course, this can also be done simply with the New Game tool on the tool bar.

Open My Game... opens a previously saved game.

Close My Game closes the game you are currently in and starts a new one.

Save My Game saves the game.

Save My Game As... saves the game with a new name or to a different disk or folder.

Print enables you to print the main screen. You might want to do this when students have a perfect game, giving them a record of their work to take home or to save in their math folders. Some teachers collect printed examples of different rectangles (like those on Student Sheets 8 and 10) to post in the classroom or to use for "find the area" problems. If the game does not print completely, select "Color/Grayscale" in the Print dialog box.

Quit gets you out of Tumbling Tetrominoes altogether, if you want to do something else on the computer or if you are ready to shut down the computer.

Saving a Game

To save a game for the first time, go to the File menu and drag down to select **Save My Game.** A dialogue box will open, in which you must name your work. Generally the best way to name a game (so you can recognize it later) is by the names or initials of the players and the date. After the name is typed in, click on the Save button.

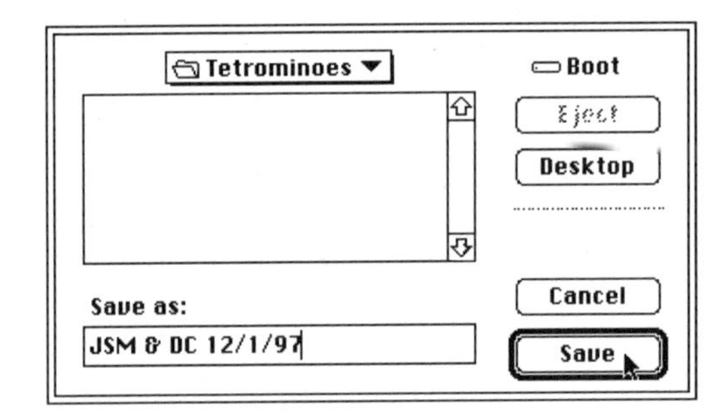

For the remainder of that session, you can save your games simply by selecting **Save** from the File menu (or pressing Command S).

If you are sharing the computer with others and it's their turn, save your game, then choose **Close My Game.** A new game will automatically open for the new players.

When you come back to the same computer later, you can start again on your saved game by selecting **Open My Game...** from the File menu. A box will appear showing all the games that have been saved. Find yours (look for your name or initials and date) and then select the name of the work you saved.

If you are the last person to use Tumbling Tetrominoes in any given session, you will want to quit the game. When you select **Quit** from the File menu, you will be asked whether you wish to save your work. If you have already saved or if you do not want to save your most recent work, click Don't Save. Otherwise, save as described above.

The Help Menu

Help
Tumbling Tetrominoes...
Tools...
Hints... ⌘H

You will find three items on the **Help** menu.

Tumbling Tetrominoes... provides basic information about the main screen and how to play the game.

Tools... explains the tools on the tool bar.

Hints... gives a series of hints for playing the game.

The Windows Menu

The **Windows** menu shows or hides the Notes window. This Notes window can be used just like a word processor, for writing things while playing the game.

For example, students might describe their strategies for placing tetrominoes, or write about the tetromino shapes that cause them the most trouble, or about discoveries they make about which size and shape of rectangle is hardest (or easiest) to fill. They might want to write a note to remind themselves how they are planning to continue a game the next day.

The Font and Style Menus

If students are using the Notes window, they might also want to use the **Font** menu and the **Style** menu. These items are simply used to change the appearance of text in the Notes window. Students may recognize the choices, which are similar to those in other word processing programs. With the **Font** menu, you can change the typeface, size, and style of your text in Notes.

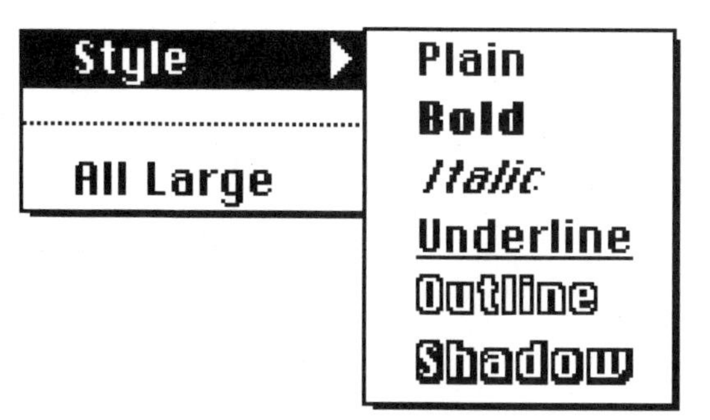

Teacher Note — Providing Appropriate Levels of Challenge

During field tests, we found large variation in the ways different classrooms and students work with Tumbling Tetrominoes. In some classrooms, students need a lot of time to get used to the computer, the motions, and the strategies involved in the game. In other classes, students master these ideas quickly and are soon ready for more difficult challenges.

If some of your students are consistently getting perfect scores, you may want to introduce one or more of the following challenges. The first two are introduced to all students in Sessions 4 and 5, but some students may be ready for them earlier.

Different Shapes Students can choose different-shaped rectangles from the tool bar. This option is introduced in Session 4 (p. 24).

Star Level Students can play at the Star level by simply clicking on the Star in the tool bar. At this level, students cannot use the Erase One tool—so if they make a mistake in placement, they're stuck. They also cannot choose the Flip motion, only Slide and Turn. This will affect the ease with which they can place some of the tetrominoes. This option is specifically introduced to the class in Session 5 (p. 28).

My Rectangle Students themselves can determine the shape and size of the rectangle to be covered, first pressing option-M to show the hidden My Rectangle tool.

Students might start by choosing a total area, then set up dimensions that would give that total. By focusing on total area first, they can explore a question like this: Is it possible to get a perfect score with any total area? For example, can you completely cover a total area of 25 (5-by-5 rectangle) with tetrominoes?

You could also have the class agree on a new total (different from 120), such as 72, and find all the possible dimensions that give that total, then experiment with these rectangles. Which of the shapes make it easy or hard to get a high score?

Superstar Game Students who are ready for a super challenge can choose the Star level and add these two additional rules: (1) They must do all their turns and left and right slides *above* the rectangle; (2) then they must "drop" each piece by choosing Slide and pressing the spacebar—thereby eliminating any chance to change their mind once they can see how the shape is going to fit. Note that these additional rules must be self-imposed and monitored by the players. Challenge them to find the best score they can make while following Superstar rules.

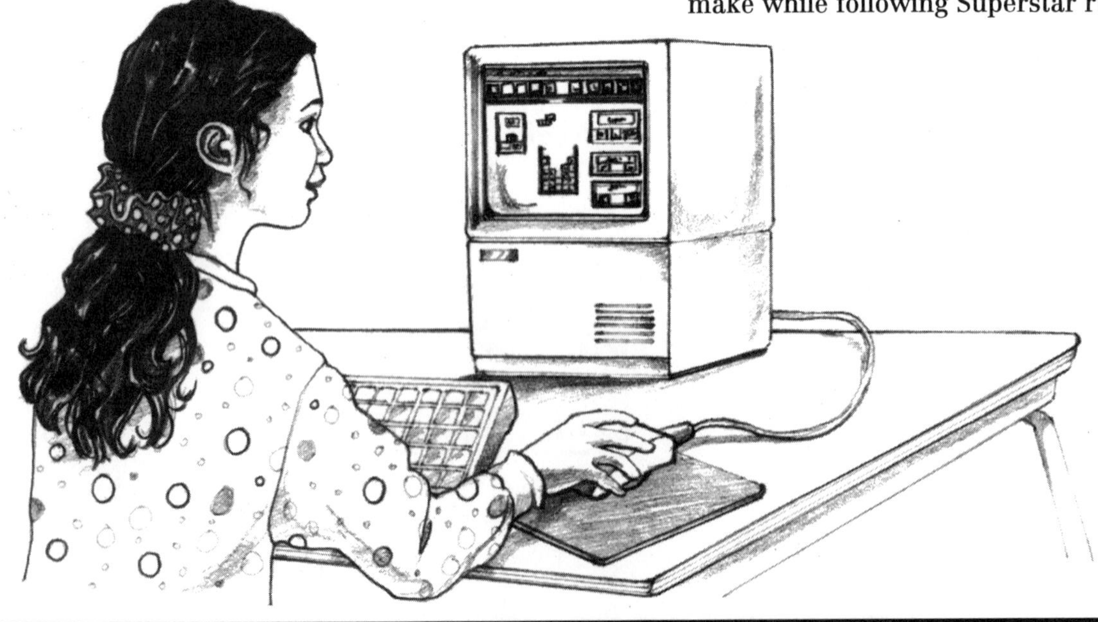

Session 4

Rectangles with Different Shapes

What Happens

Students construct different-shaped rectangles with the same area, cutting apart the 10-by-12 grids and reassembling the pieces into new rectangles. They also work on the computer game, Tumbling Tetrominoes, with different-shaped rectangles. They discuss the "fairness" of the different shapes, touching on issues about conservation of area and strategies for covering. Their work focuses on:

- comparing areas of rectangles with different dimensions
- exploring how tetromino shapes fit in rectangles with different dimensions

Materials

- 10-by-12 Rectangle (6 per pair)
- Transparent or masking tape

For the computer activity:

- Students' Game Records (from earlier sessions)

Activity

Changing the Shape of the Rectangle

We've been trying to cover our 10-by-12 rectangle with all the different tetrominoes. You found out that some of the tetrominoes will cover it perfectly, but some don't. What if we changed the shape of the rectangle? Do you think the same shapes would work, and the same shapes not work?

We're going to try that, but first we're going to make some rectangles of different shapes to work with. We're looking for rectangles that have the same total area as the 10-by-12 rectangle—120 squares—but have a different shape.

Have students work in pairs to cut apart the 10-by-12 Rectangle into parts (smaller rectangles), then tape the parts back together to make a new rectangle with a different shape, using all the pieces. Encourage students to make several different rectangles containing 120 squares.

After they make a new rectangle, students must find a way to check that it has 120 squares. If you observe them counting squares one by one, help them think about ways to count more efficiently—that is, skip counting by rows (possibly with the help of a calculator). Display the completed rectangles, labeled with their dimensions.

See the **Dialogue Box,** Changing the Rectangle's Shape (p. 26), for a sample student discussion during this activity.

When several new rectangles have been displayed, ask students to reflect on their work. This is also a good time to introduce the term *dimensions* into the conversation.

The original rectangle has 10 squares in each row and 12 rows. So, its *dimensions* are 10 by 12. What are the dimensions for the new rectangles we made? Do they have the same number of squares? How can you tell how many squares are in your rectangle without counting by ones?

Note: Be sure students save their new rectangles for Session 5, when they will try covering them with tetrominoes.

Activity

Which Shapes Are Easiest to Cover?

One of the options for Tumbling Tetrominoes, either on computer or in the paper version, is to choose a different-shaped rectangle to cover. The computer game offers several options beyond the original 12-by-10, including 10-by-12, 8-by-15, 15-by-8, 6-by-20, 20-by-6, 5-by-24, and 24-by-5.

Note: All eight options will show on 13-inch screens. On 9-inch screens, the tall 6-by-20 and 5-by-24 rectangles will not fit, so these choices will not appear on the tool bar.

For the paper version, students can use as gameboards the new rectangles they taped together at the beginning of the session.

Before they begin, ask students to think about this:

Would one shape be easier to cover completely? Which one? Let's try it and find out.

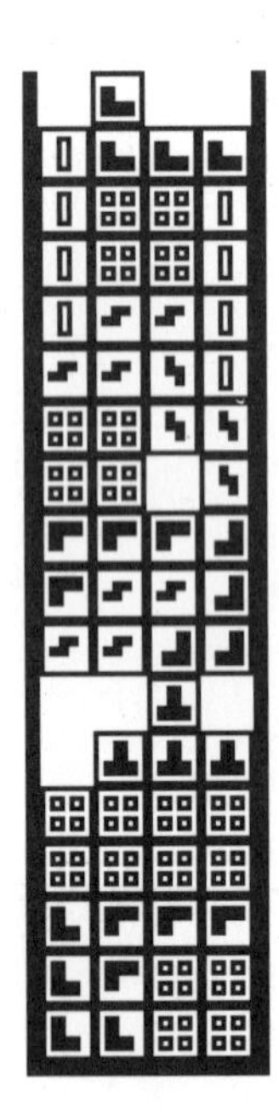

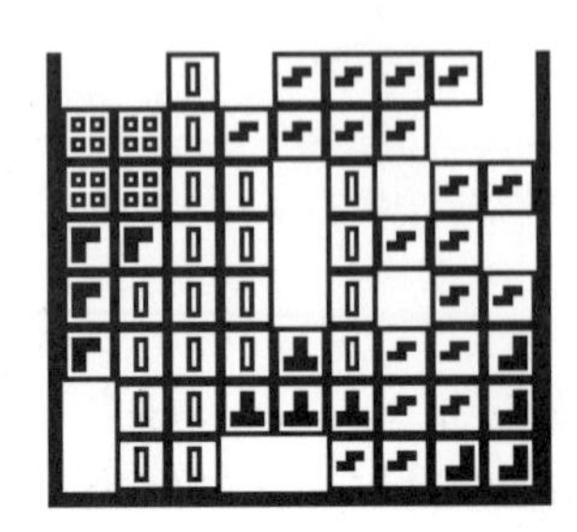

Have small groups or individuals play the game. Some students may want to save their games on the computer to show what happened when they tried new shapes. You may want to observe while they work and choose a few games to save, especially shapes that were particularly hard to fill, as examples for the class to discuss.

After everyone has tried covering new rectangle shapes, discuss the following questions with the whole class:

Are the different shapes for the rectangles all "fair"? Was it easier to completely cover some shapes and harder to cover others?

Session 4 Follow-Up

Making More Rectangles Students can take home 10-by-12 Rectangles to try making additional rectangles of different shapes but with a total area of 120 square units.

Possible Scores Students can explore the question of which scores are possible in Tumbling Tetrominoes.

Some of you got perfect scores of 120. Many got 116 or 112. Could you get a score of 119? Why or why not? What scores are possible and which are impossible?

D I A L O G U E   B O X

Changing the Rectangle's Shape

As students started the activity Changing the Shape of the Rectangle (p. 23), many at first were not sure how to make a different-shaped rectangle from the basic 10-by-12 grid. The teacher encouraged them to persist, and eventually a few solutions emerged.

The first few ideas involved cutting the 10-by-12 rectangle in half, or into strips, and taping those together. After that, most students went on to construct several different rectangles. They then discussed how to check that the total number of squares remained 120.

Do the rectangles you made have the same number of little squares—the same area—as the 10-by-12 rectangle you started with?

Ly Dinh: Mine does. Because I just cut it in half and put it back together in a different way, so it's got to have the same number.

What are the new dimensions?

Ly Dinh: It's 1, 2, 3, 4, 5, by . . . oh! It must be 5 by 24, because there's two 12's on top of each other.

Mark: That's too skinny to be 120 in all.

How else could we figure it out?

Jennifer: We could count by 5's for each row.

Liliana: We could multiply 5 times 24.

Use your way to check all the rectangles we have made. Will they all have 120 small squares?

Liliana: I'm going to get a calculator and just multiply the two dimensions on every single rectangle.

Final Challenges

What Happens

Students cover their different-shaped rectangles with tetrominoes and explore whether the same tetrominoes can cover these new rectangles as covered the original 10-by-12 grid. In the computer game, students are challenged to try the Star level, in which they cannot erase a move or flip the given shapes. As an assessment, students complete a puzzle that requires them to visualize the motions they've been using. Their work focuses on:

- reasoning about why certain shapes cover some areas, but not others
- making generalizations by examining many examples (e.g., that square tetrominoes can never fit in a rectangle with an odd dimension)
- visualizing whether two shapes are congruent

Materials

- New rectangles (from previous session and homework)
- 5-by-24 rectangles (1 per pair)
- Cubes or paper cutouts for tetrominoes
- Student Sheet 6 (1 per student)
- Glue or paste

For the computer activity:

- Students' Game Records

Activity

Covering the New Rectangles

Which tetrominoes do you think will cover perfectly the new rectangles we made? The same ones that covered the 10-by-12 rectangle? Let's try it first with a rectangle of the dimensions 5 by 24.

Hand out a 5-by-24 rectangle to each pair of students. Assign one particular tetromino to each pair (several pairs will be working with each tetromino). Have the pairs try to cover the 5-by-24 rectangle with tetrominoes of their shape made from cubes or cut from the 10-by-12 rectangle. As students work, question them about their progress.

Why did some tetrominoes that would not cover the 10-by-12 rectangle completely cover the 5-by-24 rectangle?

See the **Dialogue Box,** Tetrominoes on the 5-by-24 Rectangle (p. 30), for some examples of student reasoning. As students come to a conclusion, compile their data on the board, indicating which shapes worked for the 5-by-24 rectangle.

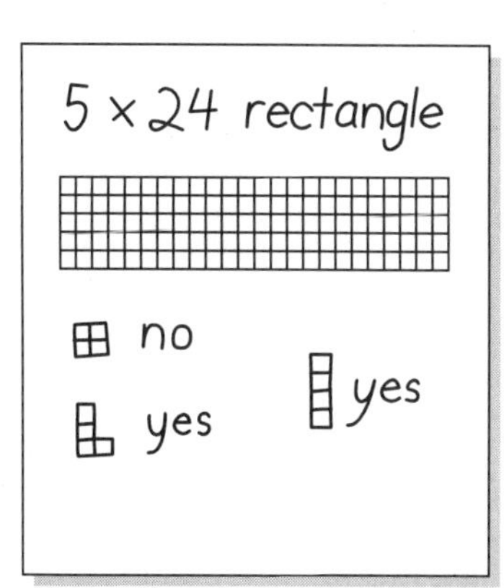

Students then try to cover one of the other new rectangles they made. They try different tetromino shapes, exploring which ones will completely cover the rectangle they've chosen. As a class, make a record of which tetrominoes fit on which rectangles and discuss these results. See the **Dialogue Box,** The T Never Fits! (p. 31), for the conclusions one class came to.

Activity

Tumbling Tetrominoes: Star Level

Once all students have had the chance to try different-shaped rectangles in Tumbling Tetrominoes on the computer, introduce the Star-level option. The challenge here is that students cannot use the Erase One tool to change a move, nor can they use the flip motion.

If you have been playing the paper version with students drawing in the tetrominoes on their gameboard, they probably have not used the "erase" possibility—it's usually too hard to erase! But if they have been using cubes or cutouts, introduce the "no changing a move" rule, and in either case introduce the "no flips" rule for Star-level play.

Have small groups or individuals play the game, on or off the computer. When they record their scores on their Game Records, they should put a star next to each score they made at the more difficult Star level.

With the whole class, discuss the following questions:

At the Star level, you can't use flips. Are flips really ever needed? Why?

Students may figure out that, without flips, certain tetrominoes cannot fit in places they *would* fit if they could be flipped.

Activity

Assessment

Puzzle Pieces

Each student completes Student Sheet 6, Puzzle Pieces. Following are some of the things you might look for in their work on this task:

- Which students are able to "see" which pieces will fit before they cut them out?
- Which students can complete the task easily, but only after cutting out the pieces? (Once they cut out the pieces, most students can place them almost immediately, showing that they are well on the way to developing visualization skills.)
- Which students can place the pieces, but only by a longer process of trial and error?
- Which students cannot determine the correct placements at all?

Students who have difficulty may need extra work on activities like the ones in this unit.

Results of this activity should be combined with everything you have observed as students have worked on this investigation to assess their understanding of congruence, motions, and area as a "covering of flat space."

Session 5 Follow-Up

Extensions

Extended Space-Covering Students can benefit from doing these space-covering games many times over the course of the year. You could post solutions, or make a book of them. Students can go on to explore rectangles of different sizes, for example, with areas of 64, 72, or 96 square units. They could also use pattern blocks to further explore patterns that cover space.

Tetris™ Some students might enjoy playing the commercial software and video game Tetris. This game also uses the tetromino shapes to cover a rectangular region, but speed is a critical factor. Challenge students to discover how the motions in Tetris differ from those in Tumbling Tetrominoes. (In Tetris, flips are not a possible move.) They may also want to discuss other differences in the goals of the games. In some classrooms, students have had interesting discussions about the pros and cons of the faster Tetris and the slower Tumbling Tetrominoes.

Exploring Factors Investigating and talking about the different dimensions (length and width) of all possible rectangles of the same area lead to interesting explorations of factors and multiples. Finding all the dimensions for rectangles with a given area results in the list of factors for that number. Area is a powerful model for visualizing multiplication and division relationships.

DIALOGUE BOX

Tetrominoes on the 5-by-24 Rectangle

In the activity Covering the New Rectangles (p. 27), small groups of students tried to cover the 5-by-24 rectangle with different tetrominoes. Following are some of the comments they made afterward.

Samir: The I tetrominoes cover it fine. You line them all up across, then you have one row at the top and you turn the rest and lay them flat [horizontally] over that row.

Chantelle: We had the 2-by-2 square tetromino. You can't do it on the 5-by-24 rectangle, because when you put two of the square tetrominoes on top of each other, you have a whole row left over. You can't fit any square tetrominoes into that row. But you can cover the 4-by-30 rectangle completely, because there's no row left over.

Cesar: We have the T tetromino. You can't do it, because you can make a big square with four T's, each turned once [90°] from each other, but that leaves a whole row out.

Kate: The Z's don't work, for the same reason they didn't work before . . . there's no way you can't leave a hole in each corner.

Aaron: The L's work, but you have to try really hard with each piece. We didn't find a pattern. We had to just keep fitting one tetromino at a time.

Maybe we can examine all the L-covered rectangles later and see if there is a pattern that works.

The T Never Fits!

2 × 60	6 × 20	5 × 24	8 × 15	3 × 40
[Z] no (29)	[L] yes (30)	[square] no	[T] no	[square] no
[tower] yes	[square] yes (30)	[tower] yes	[tower] yes	[T] no
[square] yes	[tower] yes (30)	[L] no (24)	[square] no	[tower] yes
[L] yes	[T] no (26)	[Z] no (23)	[Z] no (20)	[Z]
[T] no (29)	[Z]	[T]	[L]	[L]

For the activity Covering the New Rectangles (p. 27), a class of third graders has been finding which tetromino shapes fit in which 120-unit rectangles. Shown above are their working data (which may not be correct).

Note that their work is not yet complete—they haven't tried every shape with every rectangle. The number in parentheses tells how many tetrominoes would fit in the rectangles that they couldn't cover perfectly. Here they are discussing what they have found out so far.

Ryan: The T never fits!

Is that always true? We don't have any information for the 5-by-24.

Latisha: We're doing that one. We haven't finished yet. We did the arranging but we didn't trace it on the paper yet and we had holes.

Maria: If it's an uneven number like 5 by 24, then the squares don't work.

What do you mean by uneven numbers? I think you're on to something. I just don't understand what you mean.

Maria: Well, on the 3-by-40, squares won't work.

Jamal: On the 6-by-20, 10-by-12, and 2-by-60, it works.

Maria: And those are even numbers.

So which ones don't work?

Maria: The rectangles with the odd sides.

Su-Mei: If it's a 5 it doesn't fit, because they don't split in half.

Maria: You'd need another row to fit the squares on.

What about the L's?

Ricardo: L's are practically the same thing as squares.

What do you mean?

Ricardo: They're two lines stuck together . . . [*He sketches on the chalkboard what he means.*] So the L's don't always work.

Kate: But the towers do.

Yoshi: L's and squares and towers are the same because they can make the same shapes.

What do you mean, shapes?

Yoshi: You could put a square on top of a square and it'll be like two L's put together.

Maria: I get what he means. If you put two squares on top of each other it makes two L's.

So they'd cover the same amount of space.

Latisha: So if squares don't work, then the L's can't work either.

Maya: But I made the L's work on the 5-by-24.

Sean: You did?

Maya: Yes, it's not a pattern, but it works. I don't think L's are the same as squares and towers, because you can't juggle squares and towers around all different ways.

Sean: I don't think you can do it with L's. I want to see Maya's work.

Finding Area

What Happens

Session 1: Triangles and Squares Students use squares and triangles of unit and half-unit sizes to cover the Tetromino Puzzle. With this puzzle, they are introduced to the idea that measuring area—a flat surface—can be done by covering a surface with square units.

Sessions 2 and 3: A Poster of Four-Unit Shapes The students' primary activity is to create their own posters of many different (noncongruent) shapes with an area of four square units. Two brief (10-minute) whole-class discussions take place, one about creating new shapes from shapes students already have, the other about examining two shapes to see if they are congruent. You should schedule these two discussions as the time seems right. Students may also continue to work on Tumbling Tetrominoes.

Sessions 4 and 5: Writing About Area During these sessions, some students will be finishing up their posters and others can work at the computer on Tumbling Tetrominoes. All students work on an assessment activity in which they explain how they know that the area of a shape is 5, 6, or 7 square units.

Mathematical Emphasis

- Measuring area by covering a flat space with square units
- Comparing the area of two shapes by determining if they cover the same amount of flat space
- Comparing shapes to see if they are congruent through motions such as rotation (turns) and reflection (flips)
- Exploring relationships among shapes; for example, a rectangle can be cut into two triangles, each of which is half the area of the rectangle
- Finding the area of complex shapes by cutting them into recognizable smaller units of area, such as square units and half-units

What to Plan Ahead of Time

Materials

- Overhead projector (Sessions 1–3)
- Scissors (Sessions 1–3)
- Glue (Sessions 1–3)
- Crayons or markers (Sessions 2–3)
- Resealable plastic bags or envelopes for storage of square and triangle pieces (Sessions 2–3)
- Large paper for a poster (11-by-17-inch sheets are good): 1 per pair (Sessions 2–5)
- Computers remain available, if possible, for continued work on Tumbling Tetrominoes (Sessions 1–5)

Other Preparation

- Read the **Teacher Note,** Understanding the Area of Triangles (p. 37), before Session 1.
- You will need to make two pairs of four-unit shapes for students to compare during the second class discussion (p. 44); wait until after students have made some shapes for their posters (Session 2), and select two pairs from these. Make the shapes from cardboard or transparency film so that students will be able to turn and flip them to prove that they are or are not the same shape. (Session 3)
- Duplicate student sheets and teaching resources (located at the end of this unit) in the following quantities. If you have Student Activity Booklets, copy only the transparencies marked with an asterisk.

For Session 1

Student Sheet 7, Tetromino Puzzle (p. 68): 1 per student, and 1 transparency*

Square and Triangle Cutouts (p. 74): 1 per student, plus 5 or more per student for sessions 2–5

Student Sheet 8, What's My Score? (p. 69): 1 per student (homework)

For Sessions 2–3

Student Sheet 9, Squares! Squares! Squares! (p. 70): 1 per student (homework)

Student Sheet 10, What's My Score? What's the Area? (p. 71): 1 per student (homework)

10-by-12 Rectangle (p. 75): 2–3 per pair, and 1 transparency*

For Sessions 4–5

Student Sheet 11, Make a Shape (p. 72): 1 per student

Student Sheet 12, More 4-Unit Shapes (p. 73): 1 per student (homework)

Session 1

Triangles and Squares

Materials

- Scissors
- Glue (optional)
- Square and Triangle Cutouts (1 per student)
- Student Sheet 7 (1 per student)
- Student Sheet 8 (1 per student, homework)
- Transparency of Tetromino Puzzle
- Overhead projector

What Happens

Students use squares and triangles of unit and half-unit sizes to cover the Tetromino Puzzle. With this puzzle, they are introduced to the idea that measuring area—a flat surface—can be done by covering a surface with square units. Their work focuses on:

- exploring relationships among geometric shapes
- thinking about area as covering space

Activity

Solving the Tetromino Puzzle

Distribute to each student the Square and Triangle Cutouts, scissors, glue (if used), and Student Sheet 7, Tetromino Puzzle.

Students cut out the squares and triangles and arrange them so that they exactly cover the five tetrominoes on the puzzle sheet. Tell them they may need to arrange and rearrange to find a way to make the pieces fit.

If this is very easy for some students, ask them to put away their puzzle sheet and try to make the five tetrominoes from the square and triangle pieces, without having the outlines.

When they have all the puzzle pieces arranged, they record their solution by either gluing the pieces or drawing the outlines of the pieces in the tetrominoes on the puzzle sheet. There are many possible solutions.

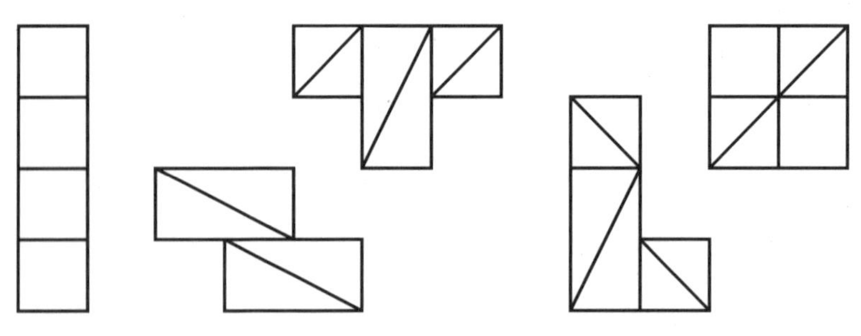

Activity

Measuring Flat Space

Introducing Area If students have had classroom experiences with measuring length, begin by referring to some of these.

Do you remember when you measured [the length of your own feet, your height]? What did you use to measure?

Listen to students' responses about how they measure something linear. Students may remember using tools such as adding machine tape, string, or rulers, using nonstandard units such as pencils ("2 pencils long"), and using standard units, such as centimeters and meters, or inches and feet.

Sometimes we want to know how long something is, like how tall you are, or how far away something is, like the distance from your house to the school. We can measure these lengths by stretching something from one end to the other, like a ruler or string.

There are also other kinds of things we need to measure. For example, we might want to figure out how big a rug must be to cover the floor, or how much wrapping paper we need to cover a box. For the rug or the wrapping paper, we want to know how much flat space something covers. We don't want to measure *just* around the edges—we want to measure *all* the space. People often measure flat space with squares, and that's what we're going to be doing.

If your classroom floor or ceiling is covered with square tiles, use these tiles as an example:

Look at our classroom floor. We could use the tiles on the floor to measure the area of the floor. How many squares do you think cover the whole floor? How could you figure that out?

Using a Unit Square to Measure Area Put the Tetromino Puzzle transparency on the overhead projector.

Sometimes people choose big squares to measure the area of a space, like the tiles on our floor. Sometimes they choose smaller squares for measuring area. Whatever the size of the square, it can be called a unit of area. For this puzzle, we are going to say that one of the small squares on this page is one unit of area.

What is the area of one of these tetrominoes? How do you know?

Students will readily agree that a tetromino has an area of four square units.

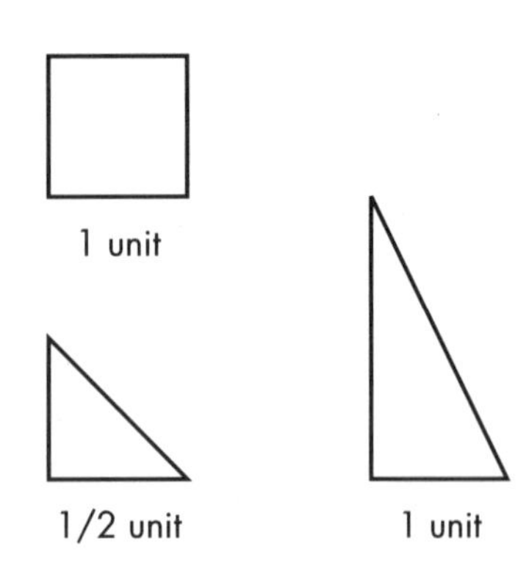

Ask students to share some of the ways they made the tetrominoes with the square and triangle puzzle pieces, drawing one at a time on the overhead or chalkboard. (You may need to provide an outline on the chalkboard.) The **Dialogue Box,** The Space Is the Same (p. 38), demonstrates how this discussion leads students to consider the idea of area as a measure of a flat surface.

As students discuss the area of these examples, they will begin to talk about the area of the half-unit triangle and the unit triangle. Ask them to explain how they know what the areas of these triangular pieces are. Encourage students to come up with different explanations. See the **Teacher Note,** Understanding the Area of Triangles (p. 37), for student reasoning you might hear and encourage. This discussion may need to be an ongoing one as students gain more experience with the two triangles.

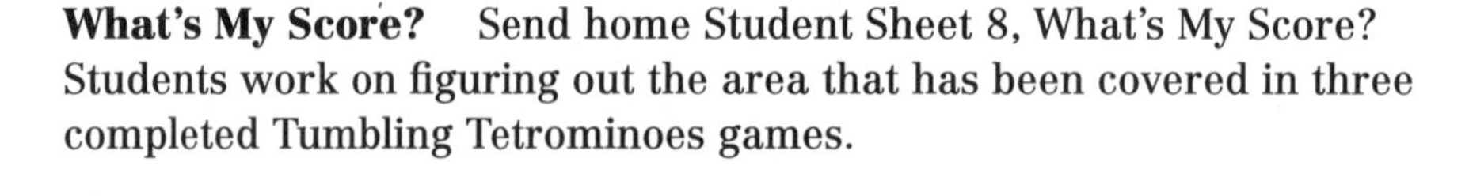

Session 1 Follow-Up

Homework

What's My Score? Send home Student Sheet 8, What's My Score? Students work on figuring out the area that has been covered in three completed Tumbling Tetrominoes games.

Extensions

Working with different-size units of area helps students understand that total area depends on what you define as one square unit. Just as a given length might be either "36 inches" or "3 feet," the measure of an area is related to the unit you choose. These extensions involve students in using other units to measure area.

Squares on the Floor If your classroom has floor or ceiling tiles, some students can pursue the question of how many squares cover the classroom floor or ceiling. If the sides of the squares are each one foot long, as many classroom floor tiles are, the unit is called a square foot. Some students may want to figure out the area of your classroom by counting the square tiles. If they investigate this question, students will grapple with such issues as these:

> Are there quicker ways to figure out the total than counting each square?
>
> How do we count partial squares, or squares we can't see?

Geoboards Geoboards use yet another size square as a unit to measure area. If you have them, students can work with their boards to make shapes with a certain area, exploring questions like these:

> What shapes can you make that have an area of 4 square units?
>
> Can you make shapes with an area of 2, 3, 4, 5, . . . square units?
>
> What is the largest shape you can make? What is its area?
>
> Can you make a shape with $2\frac{1}{2}$, $3\frac{1}{2}$, . . . square units?

Understanding the Area of Triangles

Teacher Note

Many of us learned about area only through memorizing formulas; we often did not really understand what or why we were multiplying. In this unit, students learn about measuring area as "covering a flat surface with square units." Finding the areas of triangles is done not by using a formula, but by looking at the triangle in relationship to a related rectangle. So, for example, it is easy to see that the smaller of the two triangles on the Square and Triangle Cutouts is half a square unit:

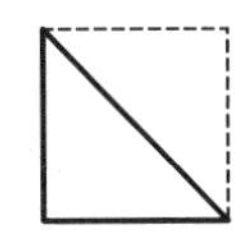

1/2 square unit

When students are comfortable with the unit square as 1 square unit and the small triangle as a half of a unit, spend time talking about the 1-unit triangle.

How do you know what the area of this shape is?

Students can use their Tetromino Puzzle to help them think about how the triangle is related to one square unit. Here are two ways to think about it: First, you can think of this shape as half of a 2-unit rectangle. Since the rectangle is 2 square units, and the triangle is half of the whole shape, we can conclude that the triangle is half of 2—or 1 square unit:

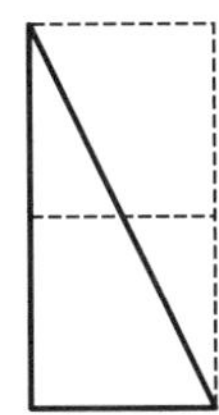

Students may express this by saying something like, "Two of them together make two squares, so each of them must be 1 unit."

Another way to see that this triangle has an area of 1 square unit is to cut the triangle into two pieces and rearrange the pieces to make a unit square.

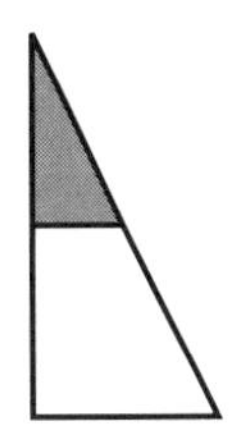

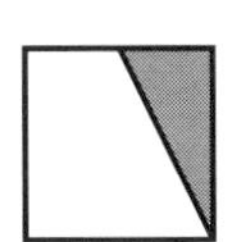

Some students will immediately "see" this relationship as they look at the unit triangle drawn on top of the 2-unit rectangle.

At this age level, some of your students may only be comfortable with the square and half-unit triangle as measures of area. This is fine. If your students do use the larger 1-unit triangle in subsequent work to make new shapes, make sure that they can prove to you what the areas of the shapes are.

For example, suppose they make the shape below (at left). A student might explain:

> See, if you cut off this piece [piece 1] and turned it around and put it over on the other side, like this [see the second figure], it would cover four squares.

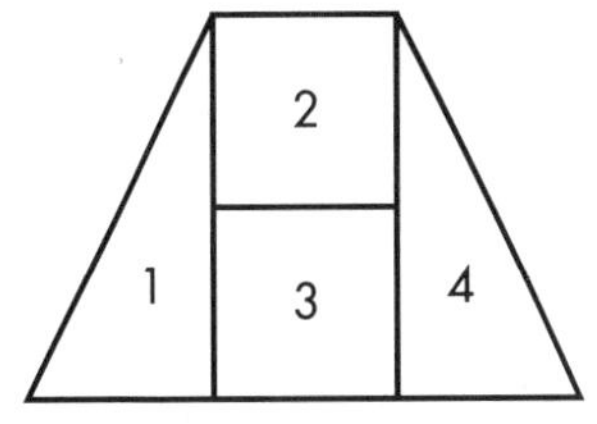

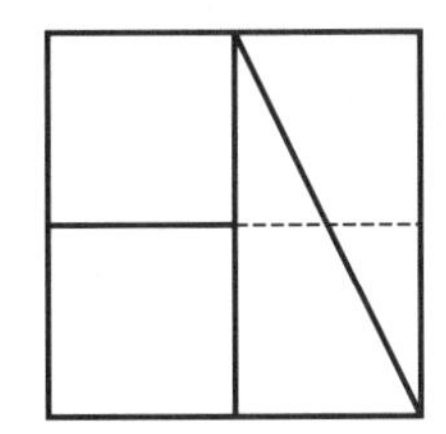

If students say only "Because this triangle is 1," they may just be parroting what they have heard from you or other students. Be sure they can explain why the area is 1 by one of the methods discussed in this note or by some other convincing method of their own.

The Space Is the Same

After students have solved the Tetromino Puzzle (p. 34) and are sharing their solutions, this class discusses the two different ways that Annie and Midori formed the square tetromino, and they consider the concept of *area*.

Annie's tetromino

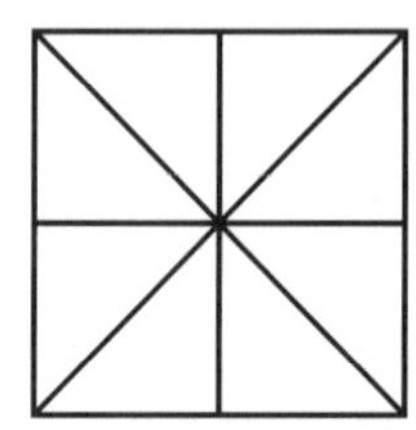

Midori's tetromino

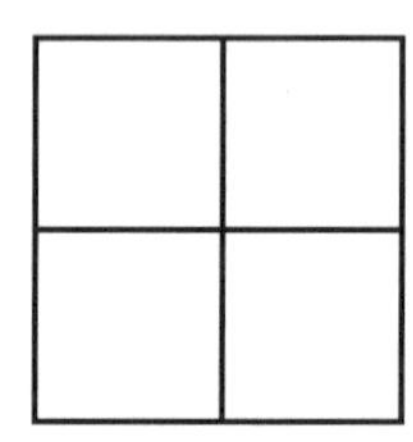

Annie: I made my square out of all the little triangles. It was twice as many—2 and 2 and 2 and 2—8 little triangles. So it has 8 areas.

But I thought Midori said that the area of her square is 4. Let's look at your square and Midori's. What do people think? Do these two have the same amount of space?

Tamara: They are the same amount, but hers has more pieces.

Tyrell: The space is the same because two of the triangles make a square, so every time it's 2, 4, 6, 8, it's really like 1, 2, 3, 4 squares.

Annie: That's what I said. It's twice as many.

Dominic: They're the same size. If you moved them, one would fit right on top of the other.

Annie, you said you made yours with twice as many pieces.

Annie: Uh-huh.

So here's my question for everybody. What's the difference between counting the number of pieces, and saying what the area—the amount of inside space—is? Or is it the same thing?

Khanh: It's like the space is the same, but she made it differently.

Laurie Jo: You can make the same amount of space different ways. You could make tiny, tiny pieces and still cover up the square. It's still the same size.

Sessions 2 and 3

A Poster of Four-Unit Shapes

What Happens

The students' primary activity is to create their own posters of many different (noncongruent) shapes with an area of four square units. Two brief (10-minute) whole-class discussions take place, one about creating new shapes from shapes students already have, the other about examining two shapes to see if they are congruent. You should schedule these two discussions as the time seems right. Students may also continue to work on Tumbling Tetrominoes. In these sessions, students' work focuses on:

- making shapes with a given area
- deciding if two shapes are congruent
- gaining experience with the relationships among squares and triangles

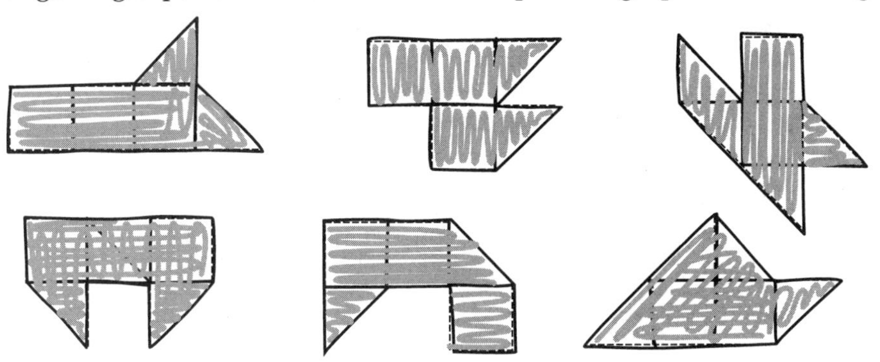

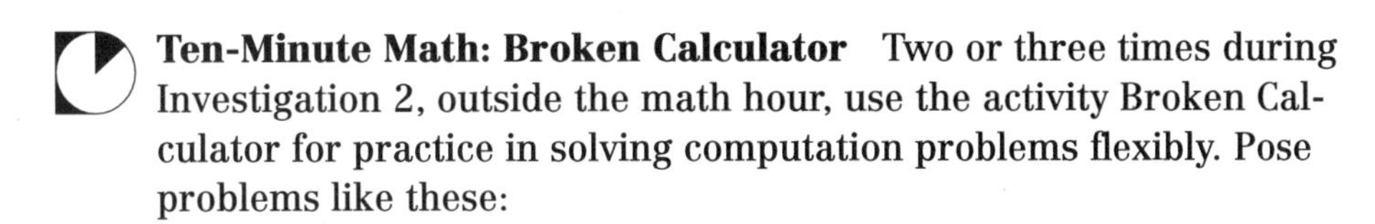

Ten-Minute Math: Broken Calculator Two or three times during Investigation 2, outside the math hour, use the activity Broken Calculator for practice in solving computation problems flexibly. Pose problems like these:

> Put 45 on your calculator screen without using the 4 or + keys.
>
> Add 103 and 111 without using 1.

After students solve the problem, list some of their solutions on the board.

Ask students to choose one solution and extend it into a series that follows a pattern. For example, to form 45 without using 4 or +:

$65 - 20 = 45$
$60 - 15 = 45$
$55 - 10 = 45$
$50 - 5 = 45$

For full directions and variations, see p. 53.

Materials

- Completed homework (Student Sheet 8)
- Overhead projector
- 10-by-12 Rectangle (2–3 per pair)
- Transparency of 10-by-12 Rectangle
- Square and Triangle Cutouts (2–3 per student)
- Resealable plastic bags or envelopes to store pieces between sessions
- Scissors, glue or paste
- Crayons or markers
- Large poster paper (1 per pair)
- Student Sheet 9 (1 per student, homework)
- Student Sheet 10 (1 per student, homework)

For the computer activity:

- Students' Game Records

Ongoing Computer Activity

During Sessions 2 and 3, some students may continue playing Tumbling Tetrominoes on the computer while others are working on the off-computer activities. You may want to introduce the game option that allows students to make and cover a rectangle of any size, within the limits of the computer screen. (This is the hidden My Rectangle tool, as explained on p. 19 in the **Teacher Note,** Directions for Tumbling Tetrominoes.) You might suggest, for example, that students make a rectangle with an area of 24 (or 36, or 48). They may need to use graph paper to first draw rectangles with the specified area, in order to discover what dimensions work.

Activity

Discussing Homework: Looking at Area

Briefly discuss the homework on Student Sheet 8, What's My Score? Students may not have thought about the Tumbling Tetrominoes game as involving area. Ask them to describe their solution strategies, and introduce the vocabulary of area into this discussion.

Suppose these rectangles from the Tumbling Tetrominoes game represented the floors of different rooms in our school, and we wanted to cover them with tiles. How many tiles would we need to cover the whole floor of each room?

How much of the area is already covered in each example? How did you figure that out?

Activity

Finding Shapes with an Area of Four Units

Hand out more copies of the 10-by-12 Rectangle and the Square and Triangle Cutouts. Students will work in pairs or threes, cutting out and then rearranging the square and triangle pieces to make many different shapes with an area of four square units.

Students already know the tetromino shapes and may want to include them, but they should also begin to generate different shapes that have an area of four square units. Explain that they are to find as many different shapes as possible to make a poster of shapes with an area of four square units. Establish two rules, using the overhead projector as needed to clarify them.

Rule 1 Each new shape must, like tetrominoes, have "full sides touching." For example, these three shapes are OK:

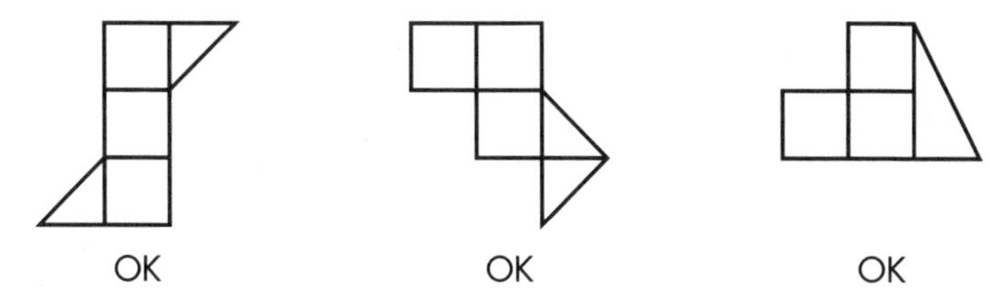

The next three shapes are *not* OK, because full sides do not always match up, or only corners are touching.

Rule 2 Each shape should be different from any others on the poster. In this case, "different" means that shapes are not congruent through rotation or reflection (turns and flips). For example, these two shapes are the same—one is a rotation of the other:

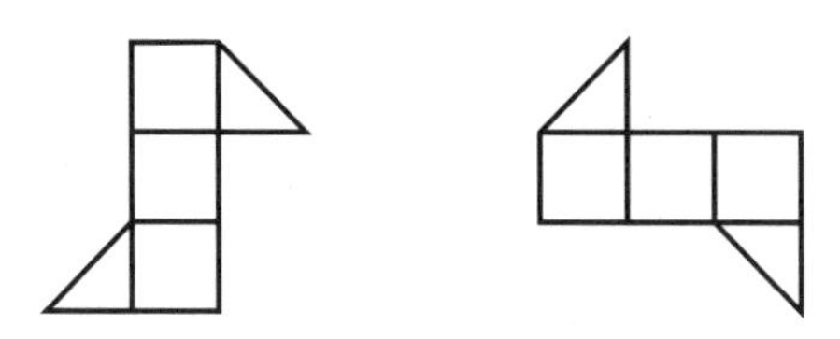

If you can lay one whole shape on top of another whole shape, it is considered the same shape. These two shapes are the same because their outline is the same, even though they were made with different pieces:

Making the Poster As each pair or small group decides they have made a new shape, they add it to the poster. There are several ways students might put together the shapes for the poster.

Some students may want to cut out the separate pieces of their shape and glue them individually onto the poster. Others may want to first build their shape with the squares and triangles, then draw the whole shape on the 10-by-12 Rectangle, color it, and cut it out to paste on the poster. Some may feel confident drawing their shape directly on the 10-by-12 Rectangle (without first building it with individual squares and triangles), then cutting it out.

When a four-unit shape is drawn and cut out as one piece, it is easier to test it for Rule 2 (to see if it is the same as any other shapes on the poster); it is also easier to glue in place. However, some shapes that can be made easily with the square and triangle pieces are quite difficult to draw on the squared paper, so students may need to use different drawing or cutting-and-pasting strategies for different shapes.

If students color in each shape, it will show up more clearly on their posters.

Note: Be alert to possible confusions that may arise in drawing the shapes on graph paper. For example, in one classroom, a student made the following shape with the square and triangle pieces, then recorded it on graph paper as shown (twice as large, with 8 square units instead of 4).

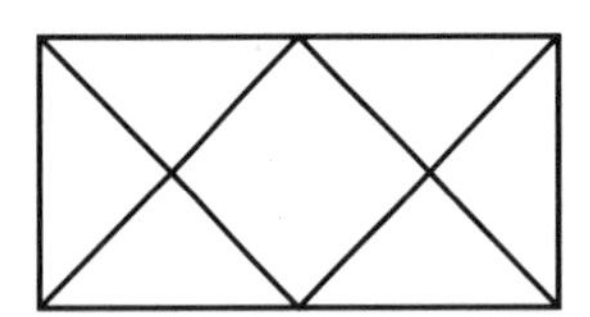

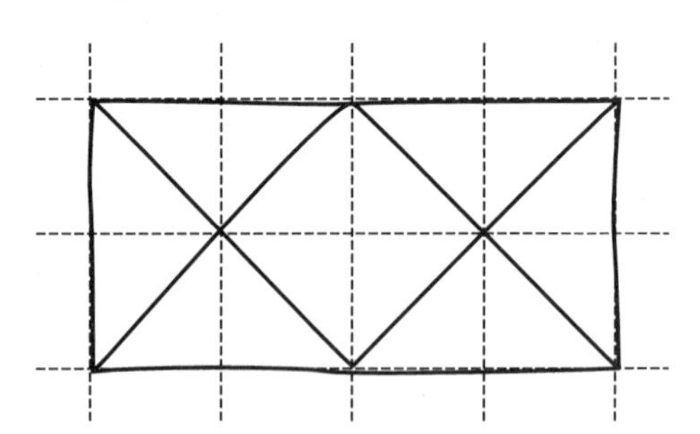

An effort to fix the mistake, to draw the shape with four square units, resulted in the drawing below (left)—four units, but no longer the unit square and half-unit triangle.

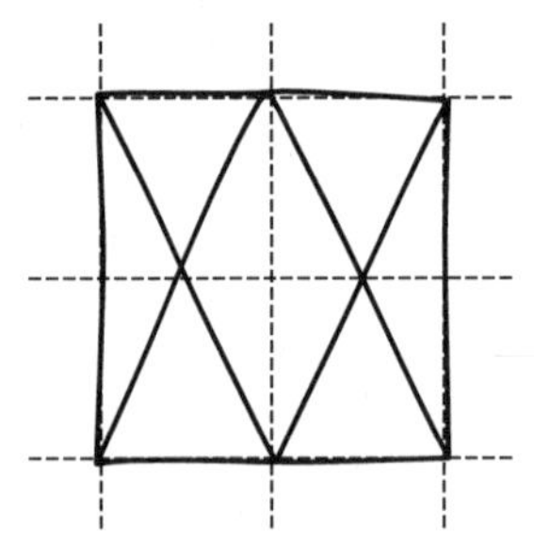

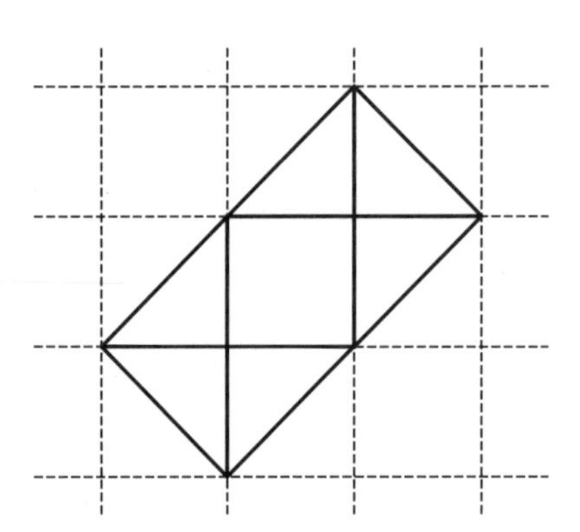

The problem is that the shape cannot be recorded on graph paper with its edges parallel to the paper; it can only be recorded on a slant (above, right). This is because the diagonal of the unit square (the long side of the triangle) is longer than the side of the square. Finding a way to record this shape could be a good challenge for the class.

Activity

Class Discussion: Creating New Shapes

This discussion works well after most students have generated three or four shapes for their posters, perhaps near the end of Session 2.

Choose a shape with an area of four square units that students have made. Outline the shape on your transparency of the 10-by-12 rectangle. Put it on the overhead, laying square and triangle pieces over the outline of the shape.

How could you change this shape a little to make a new shape?

Take students' suggestions, and have them show you the new shapes they can make by, for example, moving a single piece to a new position, or interchanging the positions of a triangle and a square. Ask other students to judge whether the new piece is different from the original piece (not congruent), for which you will still have the outline.

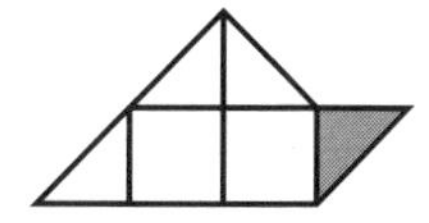
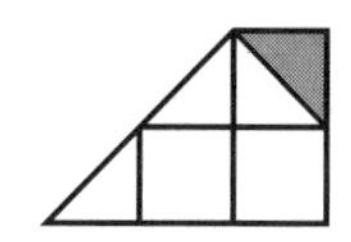
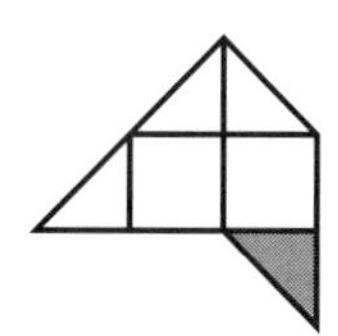
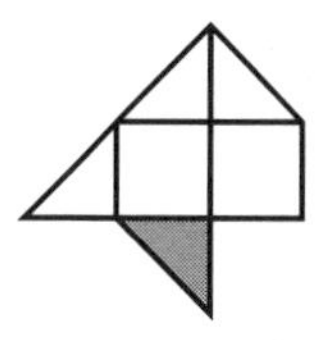

Do this again, starting with a different shape, and ask students to generate several new shapes by changing this one a little. Make sure they maintain an area of four square units.

During this discussion, also ask students if there are ways they could write numbers on the shapes to show that they contain four square units. We have seen students use two kinds of labeling to prove that their shapes are four square units:

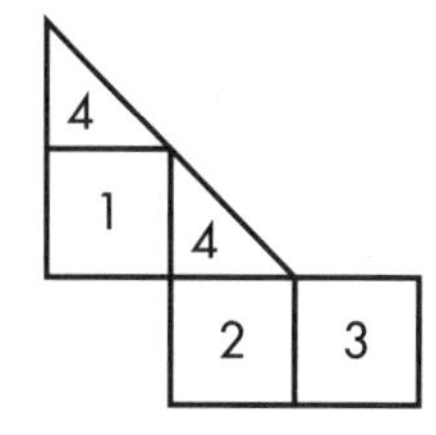

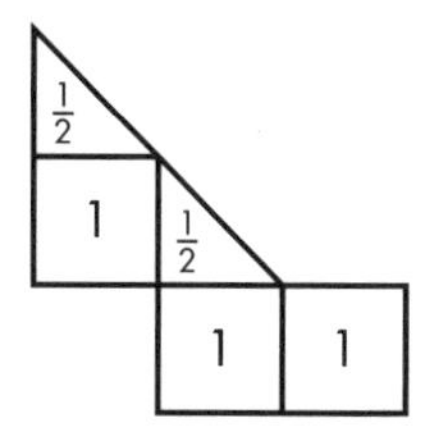

Both are good ways of showing what the area is. If students don't spontaneously use 1/2 as a way to label the half-unit triangle, this is a good time to introduce the fraction notation. You can explain it as standing for "one out of two parts," in this case, one out of the two parts of a square. Don't insist that students use this notation if they have their own adequate ways of describing the area of a shape, but continue to show student examples of both kinds of notation.

Activity

Class Discussion: Are These Two Shapes the Same?

This discussion might happen during Session 3, or whenever you have collected enough examples of four-unit-square shapes.

As you watch students work on their posters, look for congruent shapes. Don't make a point of having students eliminate duplicates. Rather, use these for a class discussion. Choose some pairs of shapes from student posters; include some pairs that are *not* congruent but look similar, and other pairs that are congruent if one is flipped or rotated.

When you have selected some pairs of shapes, cut them out of cardboard, paper, or transparency film so that, after some discussion, students will be able to actually flip and turn them to see if they are congruent. One teacher who did not have an overhead projector cut out giant shapes from cardboard and had students hold them up, turn them, and flip them to test for congruence.

Put two similar shapes at a time on the overhead (or hold them up).

Would these two shapes be the same if we flipped or turned one of them? First, see if you can tell just by looking. Why do you think the two shapes are the same (or not the same)?

Suppose, for example, that students are looking at the two pairs of shapes below.

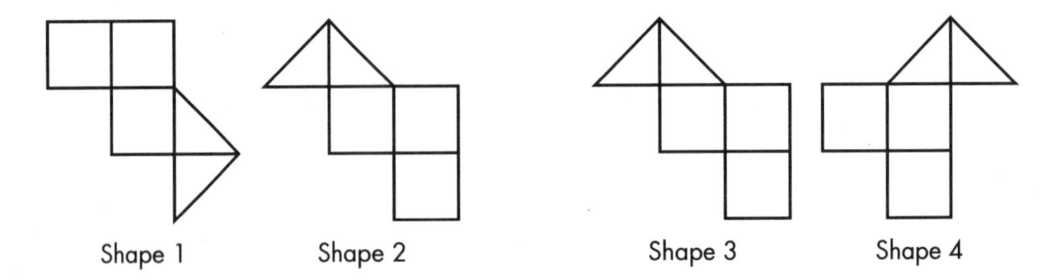

One of these pairs is not congruent, but looks like it might be. The other pair is congruent—one shape can be flipped and turned to exactly match the other. Can you tell which is which? Are shapes 1 and 2 congruent? What about shapes 3 and 4?

After some discussion, allow students to actually flip and turn the shapes to test their theories.

Sessions 2 and 3 Follow-Up

Squares! Squares! Squares! After Session 2, send home Student Sheet 9, Squares! Squares! Squares! Ask students to look for any surface in their home or neighborhood that is covered with squares. They draw a picture of the place where they found the squares and answer the questions about the area of the surface they found. This activity is a good one in which to involve family members.

What's My Score? What's the Area? After Session 3, send home Student Sheet 10, What's My Score? What's the Area? Students again figure out the area that has been covered in several completed Tumbling Tetrominoes games.

Tangrams If you have tangram puzzles, they connect well to this week's activities. Whatever figure is made from all the tangram pieces, the area is always the same.

Sessions 4 and 5

Writing About Area

Materials

- Completed homework (Sessions 2 and 3)
- Materials for finishing posters
- Student Sheet 11, Make a Shape (1 per student)
- Student Sheet 12 (1 per student, homework)
- Square and Triangle Cutouts (2 per student, homework)

For the computer activity:

- Students' Game Records

What Happens

During these sessions, students will be finishing up their posters. Some can continue to work at the computer on Tumbling Tetrominoes. All students work on an assessment activity in which they explain how they know the area of a shape is 5, 6, or 7 square units. Their work focuses on:

- making a shape with a given area
- explaining and justifying a solution in writing

Ongoing Computer Activity

During Sessions 4 and 5, students may continue playing Tumbling Tetrominoes on the computer while others are working on the off-computer activities. Working with the My Rectangle option provides further practice in determining area.

Activity

Discussing Homework: Area at Home

Take some time to ask students about the homework they did on Student Sheet 9, Squares! Squares! Squares!

Did you find areas in your homes or neighborhoods that were covered with squares? What were they? About how big was each square unit—bigger or smaller than the squares you are using for your posters? Bigger or smaller than the tiles on our classroom floor? How big was the total area (how many square units)?

You may also want to choose one of the problems on Student Sheet 10, What's My Score? What's the Area?, to discuss with the class.

What is the total area of the rectangle? How much of that area is covered? How did you figure that out?

Activity

Finishing the Posters

Students work to complete their posters of shapes with an area of four square units. As they work, they keep checking new shapes they find for congruence with shapes they already have posted. As students finish, you can display the posters in the classroom.

Some students enjoy making pictures out of their four-square-unit shapes and coloring in details and backgrounds.

Activity

Assessment

Proving the Area of a Shape

Toward the end of Sessions 4 and 5, hand out Student Sheet 11, Make a Shape. Have each student draw a shape that is 5, 6, or 7 square units in area, using the dotted grid as a guide. Encourage students to use all three kinds of shapes they have worked with in this unit: the unit square, the half-unit triangle, and the unit triangle.

After drawing their shape, the students write an explanation of how they know what its area is. When you give students this assignment, explain that they may be doing several drafts, just as they do when they write, until they have a finished piece of work.

As students show you their written work, make sure that they have a complete explanation that could be understood by someone who had not been in class. Ask clarifying questions and have students add what they tell you to their written work. The **Dialogue Box,** The Area of My Shape Is 5 (p. 52), shows how a teacher encouraged one student to clarify her explanation in successive drafts.

❖ **Tip for the Linguistically Diverse Classroom** Students who are not yet writing in English can share how they know their shape has a specific area by creating a visual math problem. For example:

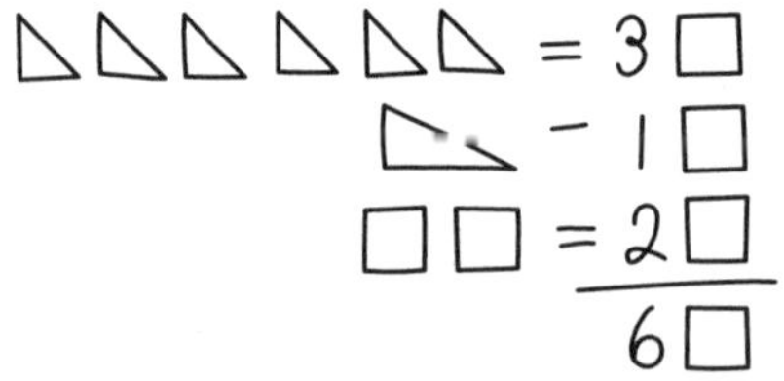

△△△△△△ = 3 □
△ - 1 □
□□ = 2 □
6 □

For the revision, encourage students to add to their drawings to explain even further. For example:

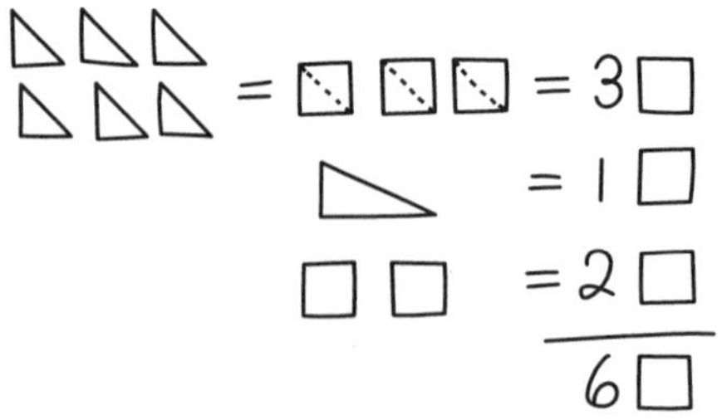

△△△
△△△ = ⧅ ⧅ ⧅ = 3 □
△ = 1 □
□□ = 2 □
6 □

You may want to assign this task for homework after Session 4, then give students time in class to revise it during Session 5. For discussion about how to evaluate this assessment, see the **Teacher Note,** Assessment: Proving the Area of a Shape (p. 50).

Activity

Choosing Student Work to Save

As the unit ends, you may want to use one of the following options for creating a record of students' work on this unit.

- Students look back through their folders or notebooks and write about what they learned in this unit, what they remember most, what was hard or easy for them. You might have students do this work during their writing time.
- Students select one or two pieces of their work as their best work, and you also choose one or two pieces of their work to be saved in a portfolio for the year. You might include the last assessment in the unit, Proving the Area of a Shape (Investigation 2, Session 5), and any other assessment tasks from this unit. Students can create a separate page with brief comments describing each piece of work.
- You may want to send a selection of work home for parents to see. Students write a cover letter, describing their work in this unit. This work should be returned if you are keeping a year-long portfolio of mathematics work for each student.

Sessions 4 and 5 Follow-Up

More 4-Unit Shapes After session 4, send home Student Sheet 12, More 4-Unit Shapes, and 2 copies of Square and Triangle Cutouts. Students cut out the squares and triangles and use them to generate new shapes with exactly 4 square units. They might add any new and interesting shapes they make at home to their posters.

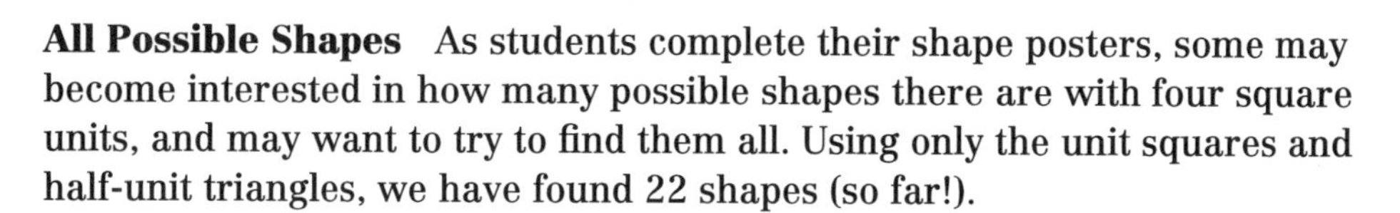

All Possible Shapes As students complete their shape posters, some may become interested in how many possible shapes there are with four square units, and may want to try to find them all. Using only the unit squares and half-unit triangles, we have found 22 shapes (so far!).

You might compile a class poster showing all the different shapes that the class has discovered, with no duplicates. This compilation can remain displayed beyond the completion of this unit, and students can continue to try to find new shapes.

Remember, a shape that is a flip or rotation of another shape is considered the same. Students need to carefully compare any "new" shape to the shapes that have already been created.

Teacher Note — Assessment: Proving the Area of a Shape

This assessment asks students to solve a problem, justify their solution, and then write about their work. Communicating about mathematical reasoning is difficult, especially if students have not had much experience doing so. However, it is a critical part of mathematical activity. Because writing is difficult for many students, we treat this task in the way that we treat any writing assignment—giving students time to write down their first thoughts, present these to an audience (you), get feedback on their work, and then use that feedback to revise it.

It is important that students' performance not be judged only on their first attempts at solving a problem, but that they be given time to think, reflect, and revise.

As you look at your own students' work, these questions can help guide your assessment:

- Was the student able to draw a shape and clearly show its area?
- Did the student understand how much area the half-unit and unit triangles covered?
- Was the student able to explain clearly how to calculate the area?

Following are several examples of student work. The first two explanations, Khanh's and Elena's, are quite clear and inclusive.

Khanh's writing:
I know that there are 5 because 2 triangles make 1 square exactly. And 1 square makes 1, and my design has 6 triangles, and 6 triangles make 3, and 2 squares make 2, and 3 plus 2 makes 5 square units.

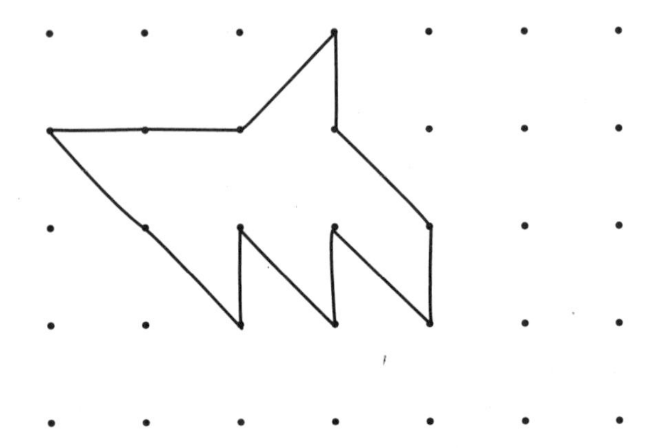

Elena's writing:
There are 4 of the little triangles. That's 4 halves, so that makes 2. Then there's 2 of the big triangles. If you put them together like I did they cover two squares, so that's 2 more. That's 4 so far. Then there's 2 regular squares. So 2 more makes 6 squares.

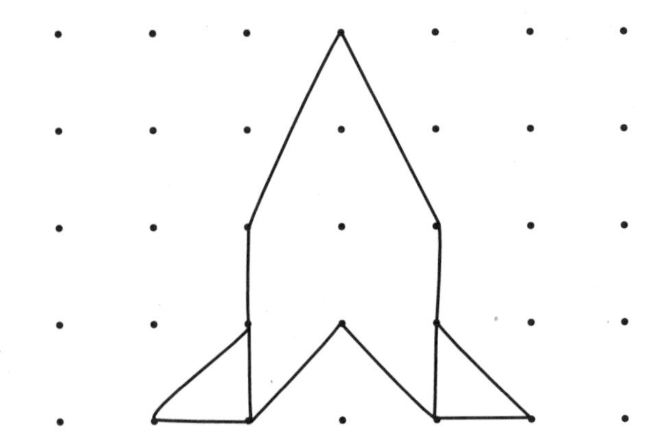

Both Khanh and Elena demonstrate their knowledge of the relationships between triangles and squares, and explain how to combine the pieces to find the area of their shapes. Elena has set herself a somewhat harder task, including the unit triangle in her shape.

Here are two examples of less complete explanations:

Jeremy's writing:
I know that my shape has 6 square units because it has 2 squares and 8 triangles and when you add them together you get 6 square units.

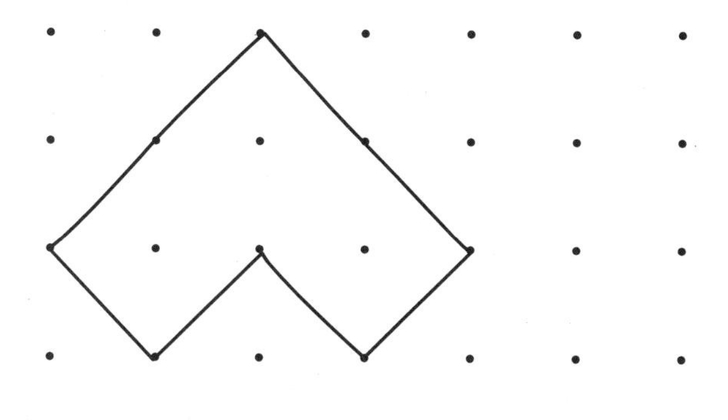

Laurie Jo's writing:
I counted them in halves and in wholes. The triangles are the halves and the wholes are the squares.

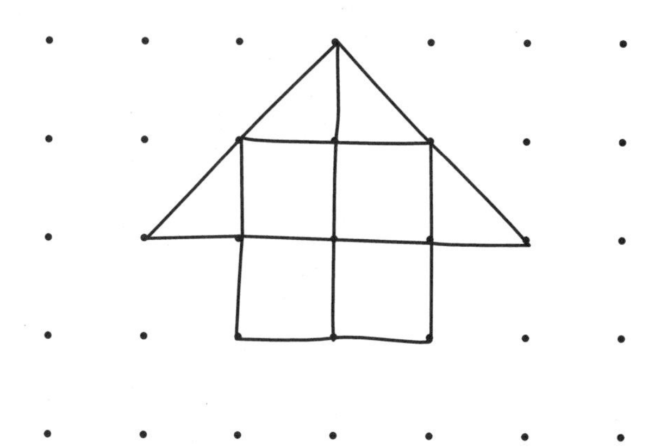

Jeremy and Laurie Jo may have a clear understanding of how to use the squares and triangles to measure the area of their shapes, but they have difficulty writing down their explanations. Further questioning might determine if these students are just repeating that triangles are halves because everyone is saying that, or if they are able to explain why this is true.

Mark's writing:
There are three squares and four triangles.

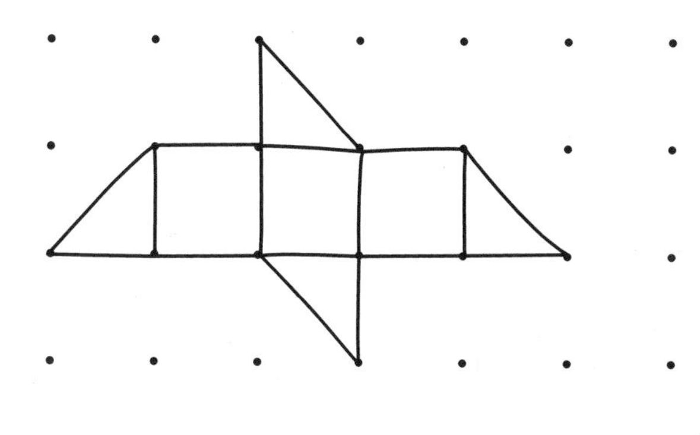

Amanda's writing:
Because it's different and I like it.

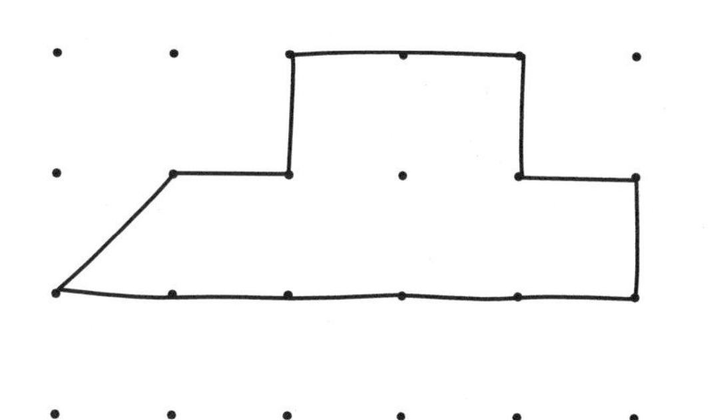

When students have a much less adequate explanation, this may indicate that they are not yet thinking about area as a covering of flat space. Mark and Amanda might need more guidance along those lines.

Amanda's writing could be a sign that she doesn't understand what you mean when you ask her to write about her mathematical thinking. She may be answering a question like "What did you think of this problem?" Further conversation is needed to determine what she understands about the problem itself.

The Area of My Shape Is 5

Seung created a 5-unit shape for the assessment activity, Proving the Area of a Shape (p. 48). When Seung showed her work to her teacher, the following discussion helped the girl clarify her writing.

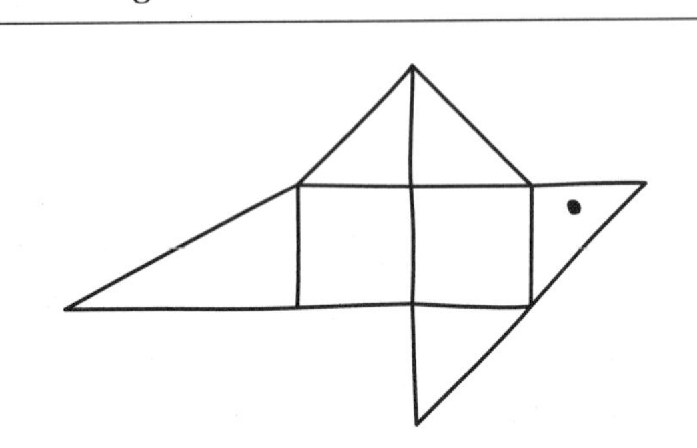

my fish. I know that the area of my fish is 5 because it has two squares and 4 triangles and 1 big triangle.

Why does 2 squares and 4 triangles and 1 big triangle make 5 square units? Maybe someone would count the pieces, [*pointing to the pieces in succession*] **1, 2, 3, 4, 5, 6, 7, and say that the area is 7.**

Seung: No, because the squares are 1, 2, and then each triangle is half.

So how does that work to make 5?

Seung: Because, see, 1, 2 [*touching each square*], 3 [*touching two small triangles*], 4 [*touching the other two small triangles*], and 5 [*touching the large triangle*].

So you need to write more about how you counted the area.

Seung then added to her writing, so that it read:

my fish. I know that the area of my fish is 5 because it has two squares and 4 triangles and 1 big triangle. The squares make two and then two triangles make one more and the other two triangles make one more, so that's 4. Then the one big triangle is a 1, so that makes 5!

That makes it much clearer to someone reading this how you counted the area to be 5 square units altogether. I only have one more question: How do you know that two small triangles make one square unit and the big triangle by itself is one square unit?

Seung protested that she knew "because we've been doing it all the time," but the teacher explained that her solution should make sense to someone who hadn't been "doing it all the time."

Seung's final writing looked like this:

my fish. I know that the area of my fish is 5 because it has two squares and 4 triangles and 1 big triangle. The squares make two and then two triangles make one more and the other two triangles make one more, so that's 4. Then the one big triangle is a 1, so that makes 5! Two small triangles make one square because if you put them together, they make one, like this:

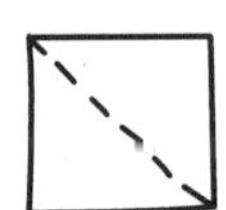

The big triangle is the same as 1 square because if you chop off the top and attach it to the bottom, it's the same.

Broken Calculator

Basic Activity

Students work to get an answer on their calculator display while pretending that some of the keys are missing. The missing keys can be operations, numbers, or both. After students find one solution, they find others by making a small change in the first one. In this way, the solutions form a pattern.

Broken Calculator helps students develop flexibility in solving problems. They pull numbers apart and put them back together in a variety of ways as they look for expressions to substitute for given numbers. Students focus on:

- finding alternative paths to an answer when a familiar one isn't available
- finding many ways to get one answer
- writing related problems

Materials

Calculators: 1 per student

Procedure

Step 1. Pose the problem. For example, "I want to make 35 using my calculator, but the 3 key and the 5 key are broken. How can I use my calculator to do this task?"

Step 2. Students solve the problem by themselves. They record their solution in some way that another student can understand. Students in small groups check each others' solutions on their calculators.

Step 3. List some of the students' solutions on the board. For example, here are some possible solutions to making 35 without the 3 and 5 key:

$61 - 26$ $29 + 6$ $4 \times 9 - 1$

Step 4. Students choose one solution and extend it, making a series of related solutions. For example:

$61 - 26$	$29 + 6$	$2 \times 18 - 1$
$62 - 27$	$28 + 7$	$4 \times 9 - 1$
$64 - 29$	$27 + 8$	$6 \times 6 - 1$
	$26 + 9$	
	$24 + 11$	

Students check each others' solutions and find another solution that follows the same pattern.

Variations

Restricting Number Keys

- Students make numbers without using the digits in those numbers, for example:

  Make 1000 without using a 1 or a 0.

  $998 + 2$
  $997 + 3$
  $996 + 4$

- Students make decimals without using the decimal point. Start with the simplest ones (0.1, 0.5, 0.25, 0.75, or 1.5) only after students have some experience relating them to fractions and division. You might start by providing a solution or two and challenge them to find some more: "I can make 0.5 on my calculator by using the keys $1 \div 2$. Why do you think that works? Can you find another way to make 0.5?"

  Some solutions for making 0.5 are $2 \div 4$, $3 \div 6$, $4 \div 8$, $5 \div 10$, $100 \div 200$, $1000 \div 2000$.

Restricting Operation Keys

- Students make a number using only addition. If you suggest a large number, students can make use of landmark numbers. For example:

  Make 2754.

$2000 + 700 + 54$	$2750 + 4$	$2749 + 5$
$2000 + 600 + 154$	$2751 + 3$	$2748 + 6$

Continued on next page

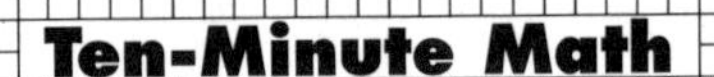

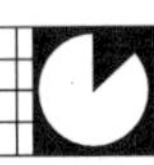

- Students make a number using only subtraction. Present the challenge of getting a number on the display using only subtraction. The +, ×, ÷ keys are broken. Patterns of solutions for making 8 might look like these:

20 – 12	1008 – 1000
19 – 11	908 – 900
18 – 10	808 – 800
17 – 9	708 – 700

- Students make a number using only multiplication and division. The + and – keys are broken. Pick numbers that have many factors. Answers for making 24 might be:

1 × 24	24 ÷ 1	24 × 1 ÷ 1
2 × 12	48 ÷ 2	24 × 2 ÷ 2
3 × 8	72 ÷ 3	24 × 3 ÷ 3
4 × 6		24 × 4 ÷ 4

(One student filled a page with the third series so he could say he'd gotten the most answers.)

Restricting Both Operations and Digits

- Make the missing operations problems more challenging by also not allowing students to use any of the digits in the final number. For example:

  Make 654 using only addition and subtraction, and without using the digits 6, 5, or 4

Related Homework Option

Pose one or two Broken Calculator problems only. Challenge students to solve the problems in more than one way, and to make their different solutions follow a pattern. They should write down their solutions so that another student can read them and know what to do on the calculator.

If students do not have calculators at home, give them time to try out their solutions the next day in school.

The following activities will help ensure that this unit is comprehensible to students who are acquiring English as a second language. The suggested approach is based on *The Natural Approach: Language Acquisition in the Classroom* by Stephen D. Krashen and Tracy D. Terrell (Alemany Press, 1983). The intent is for second-language learners to acquire new vocabulary in an active, meaningful context.

Note that *acquiring* a word is different from *learning* a word. Depending on their level of proficiency, students may be able to comprehend a word upon hearing it during an investigation, without being able to say it. Other students may be able to use the word orally, but not read or write it. The goal is to help students naturally acquire targeted vocabulary at their present level of proficiency.

We suggest using these activities just before the related investigations. The activities can also be led by English-proficient students.

Investigation 1

copy, copies, L, T

1. Draw an L shape on a piece of graph paper. Identify the shape by name, and relate it to the English alphabet.

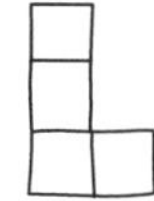

   Then make two or three copies of exactly the same shape elsewhere on the graph paper. As you do so, explain that you are making *copies* of the L shape. Emphasize and show how each *copy* looks exactly like the original. Repeat the procedure with a T shape.
2. Challenge students to demonstrate comprehension of these words by following action commands. Draw an L shape and a T shape on the board. Ask students to come make a *copy* or several *copies* of the one you name.

motion, slide, flip, turn

1. Give each student four tetrominoes made from interlocking cubes, two L-shaped and two T-shaped. Explain and demonstrate the three different motions (slide, flip, turn) with these cubes.
2. Invite students to follow your motions as you flip, slide, and turn the tetrominoes. Be sure to articulate each motion as you demonstrate it.

   Flip your L shapes.
   Turn your L shapes to look like a bed.
   Slide all your shapes together so they are touching.
3. Ask questions that challenge students to slide, flip, or turn their tetrominoes to create new shapes.

   What motions will make the two L-shapes into a rectangle?
   What motions will make the two T-shapes into the letter I?

   Students can give one-word responses or demonstrate their answers. If they choose to demonstrate, identify each motion as the student makes it.

   Cesar flips one of his L-shapes. Now he slides it so it is touching the other one.

pieces, cover, fit

1. Give students squares cut from paper (you might cut apart the 10-by-12 Rectangle, p. 75).
2. Show students a cutout rectangle, about 5 by 4 inches. Tell them you are going to *cover* it with a book. As you do so, point out that they can no longer see any of the rectangle once it has been covered.
3. Point to the cut-out squares. Ask if all these *pieces* will *fit* on the rectangle, without any overlapping. Students can experiment to find out. Ask them to count how many pieces actually fit. Also ask if the pieces *cover* the rectangle.
4. Repeat the activity with rectangles of different dimensions.

possible, impossible

1. Give each student 5 interlocking cubes. Draw and identify a 2-by-2 square on the board.

   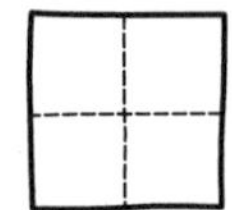

   Nod as you explain that it's *possible* to use some of the cubes to make this shape. Ask a student to demonstrate how.

2. Draw a 2-by-4 rectangle and a circle on the board.

    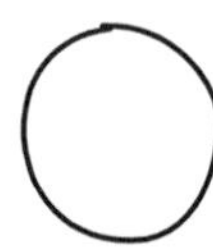

   Challenge a student to make these shapes with the cubes. Shake your head as you say it is *impossible* to do so.

3. Continue drawing different shapes (such as a triangle, a T, an oval, an L). As you point to each one, ask students whether it is *possible* or *impossible* to use the 5 cubes to make that shape. Students can answer with the words *possible* and *impossible,* or simply by nodding yes and shaking their heads no. If students are unsure, give them time to experiment.

4. Draw the "possible" shapes students have identified, and ask if those are *all* the possible shapes that can be made with 5 cubes. If not, ask the students to show you other shapes that are possible.

score

1. Show recent newspaper clippings with scores of games (using whatever sport is in season). Identify the *score* as the number of points the teams made in the game.

2. Challenge students to a simple game such as tic-tac-toe or Scissors, Paper, Rock. On the board, write two headings: MY SCORE and YOUR SCORE. At the end of each round, make a tally mark in the appropriate column. After each round, verbalize the present score.

   You just won. The score is now 1 to 0.

3. After a preset number of rounds (about 6 to 10), have students add up the final score.

The disk packaged with this *Flips, Turns, and Area* unit contains the Tumbling Tetrominoes program and a Read Me file. You may run the program directly from this disk, but it is better to put a copy of Tumbling Tetrominoes on your hard disk and store the original disk for safekeeping. Putting a program on your hard disk is called *installing* it.

To install the contents of the Tumbling Tetrominoes disk on your hard disk, follow these steps (or the instructions with your Macintosh computer).

1. Lock the Tumbling Tetrominoes program disk by sliding up the black tab on the back, so that the hole is open. The Tumbling Tetrominoes disk is your master copy of the program. Locking the disk allows copying it while protecting its contents.

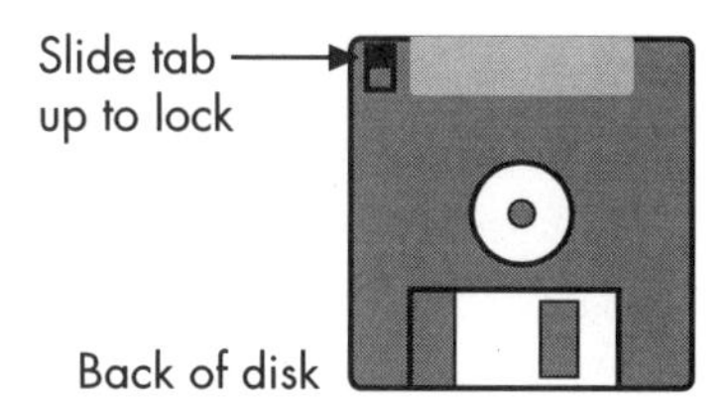

2. Insert the Tumbling Tetrominoes disk into the floppy disk drive.
3. Double-click the icon of the Tumbling Tetrominoes disk to open it.
4. Double-click to open and review the Read Me file for any recent changes in how to install or use the program. Click in the Close box after reading.
5. Click on and drag the Tumbling Tetrominoes disk icon (the outline moves) to the hard disk icon until the hard disk icon is highlighted, then release the mouse button.

Messages will appear, indicating that the contents of the Tumbling Tetrominoes disk are being copied to the hard disk. The copy will be in a folder on the hard disk with the name "Tumbling Tetrominoes."

6. Eject the Tumbling Tetrominoes disk by dragging it to the Trash. (Don't worry, the disk will not be erased.) Store the disk in a safe place.
7. If the hard disk window is not open on the desktop, open it by double-clicking on the hard-disk icon. The hard disk window will appear, showing you the contents of your hard disk. It might look something like this.

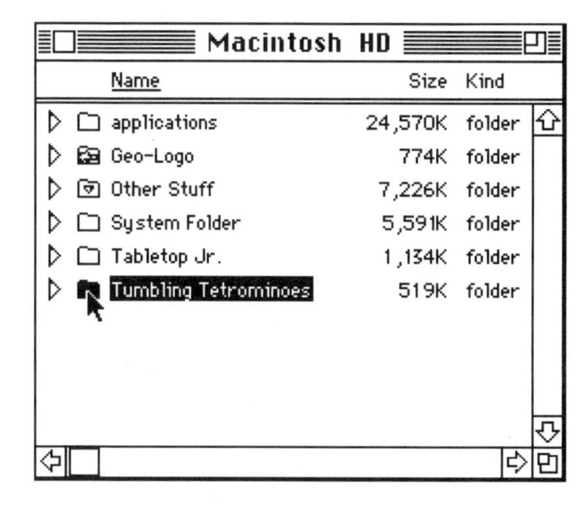

You should see the folder labeled Tumbling Tetrominoes, holding the contents of the Tumbling Tetrominoes disk.

8. Double-click the Tumbling Tetrominoes folder to select and open it. When you open this folder, the window shows the program your students will be using with this unit. It may look like this:

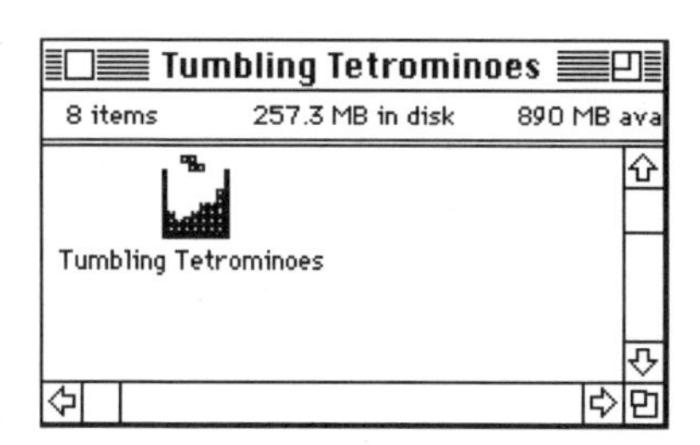

To select and run Tumbling Tetrominoes, double-click on the program icon.

Optional Use of Alias

For ease at startup, you can create an alias for the Tumbling Tetrominoes program by following these steps:

1. Select the program icon.
2. Choose **Make Alias** from the **File** menu. The alias is connected to the original file that it represents, so when you open an alias, you are actually opening the original file. This alias can be moved to any location on the desktop.
3. Move the Tumbling Tetrominoes alias out of the window to the desktop space under the hard disk icon.

For startup, double-click on the Tumbling Tetrominoes alias. This is simply a shortcut that saves you from having to open first the hard disk and then the Tumbling Tetrominoes folder to start the program inside.

Troubleshooting

This section contains suggestions for how to correct errors, how to get back to what you want to be doing when you are somewhere else in the program, and what to do in some troubling situations. If you are new to using the computer, you might also ask a computer coordinator or an experienced friend for help.

Nothing happens after double-clicking on the Tumbling Tetrominoes icon.

- If you are sure you double-clicked correctly, wait a bit longer. Tumbling Tetrominoes takes a while to open or load, and nothing new will appear on the screen for a few seconds.
- On the other hand, you may have double-clicked too slowly, or moved the mouse between your clicks. In that case, try again.

Windows or tools dragged to a different position by mistake.

Drag the window back into place by following these steps: Place the pointer arrow in the stripes of the title bar. Press and hold the button as you move the mouse. An outline of the window indicates the new location. Release the button and the window moves to that location.

I clicked somewhere and now Tumbling Tetrominoes is gone! What happened?

You probably clicked in a part of the screen not used by Tumbling Tetrominoes, and the computer took you to another application or to the "desktop."

- Click in the Tumbling Tetrominoes window or select it from the desktop.

System Error Message

Some difficulty with the Tumbling Tetrominoes program or your computer caused the computer to stop functioning. Turn off the computer and repeat the steps to turn it on and start Tumbling Tetrominoes again. Any work that you saved will still be available to open from your disk.

I tried to Print and nothing happens.

- Check that the printer is connected and turned on.
- When printers are not functioning properly, a system error may occur, causing the computer to "freeze." If there is no response from the keyboard or when moving or clicking with the mouse, you may have to shut down the computer and start over. See System Error Message, above.
- Check that "Color/Grayscale" is selected in the Print dialog box.

Blackline Masters

______________________, 19 ____

Dear Family,

Our class is beginning a mathematics unit called *Flips, Turns, and Area.* The ideas in this unit may be new to you. Your child will learn about special shapes called *tetrominoes*—different arrangements of four squares:

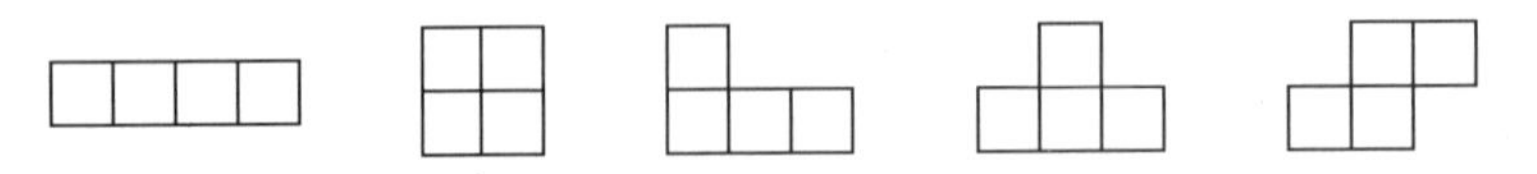

We'll be talking about three ways we can move these shapes—

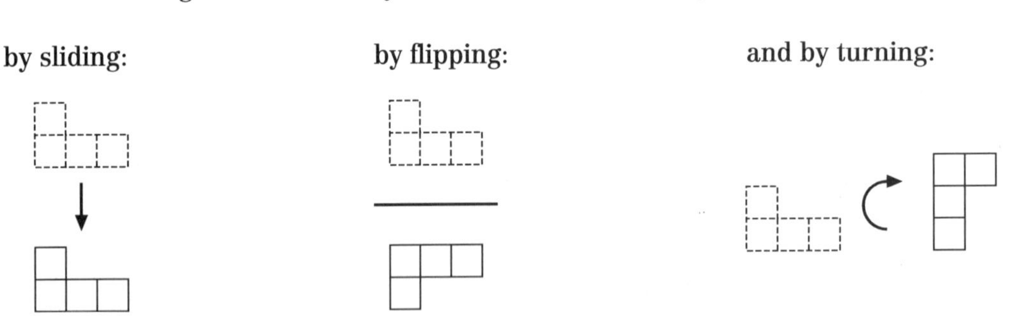

We'll work with these ideas using paper cutouts and a computer game called Tumbling Tetrominoes. After we've started the unit, ask your child to explain the game to you.

Being able to visualize how different shapes fit in space is an important geometric skill. It also has a lot of practical aspects. For example, think of how hard it is to get a couch up a stairway and into the living room—it's really a matter of slides, flips, and turns!

Part of this unit is about discovering *area* as a measure of a flat surface. Look for opportunities at home to talk about area with your child. For example:

> Do you have square tiles covering a floor or bathroom wall? How many squares are there?
>
> Suppose you make roll-out cookies with your child. This poses a problem of area: How can you place the cookie cutters so that you cover the most area, and have the least amount of dough leftover? Do you have to rotate the cookie cutter to get the best fit?

Have a good time exploring these ideas with your child!

Sincerely,

Name Date

Student Sheet 1

Making Tetrominoes

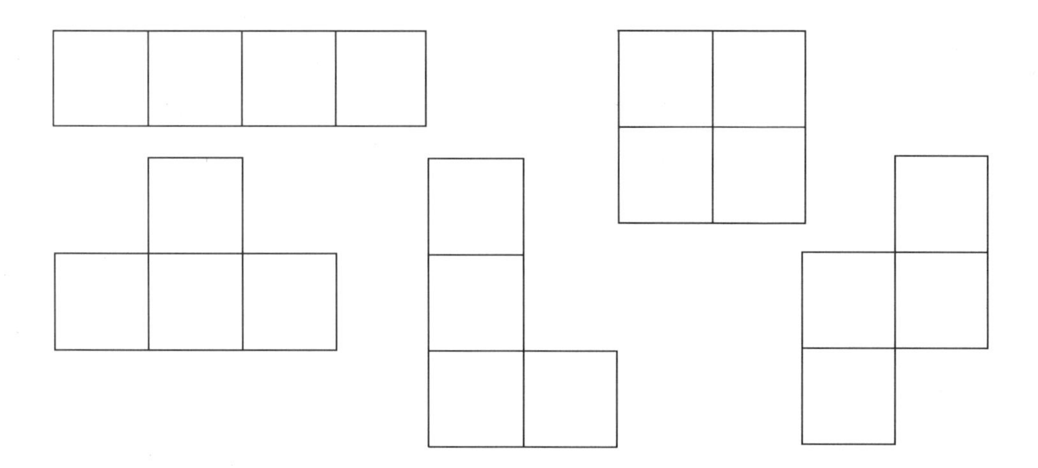

Choose your favorite tetromino shape.
Use the 10-by-12 Rectangle to make many copies of that one shape. You will use your shapes to cover rectangles.

Color each tetromino. Make all the squares in one tetromino the same color. But you can use lots of colors. You could make a red tetromino, a blue tetromino, a purple tetromino, and so forth.

Cut out each tetromino. If you don't have scissors at home, you can cut out the tetrominoes in class. Store your tetrominoes in a bag or envelope.

Count them. Write the number you have, and keep it with your shapes.

You need to make at least 30. If you don't finish, you will have time to make more in class.

Name Date

Student Sheet 2

How to Play Tumbling Tetrominoes (page 1 of 2)

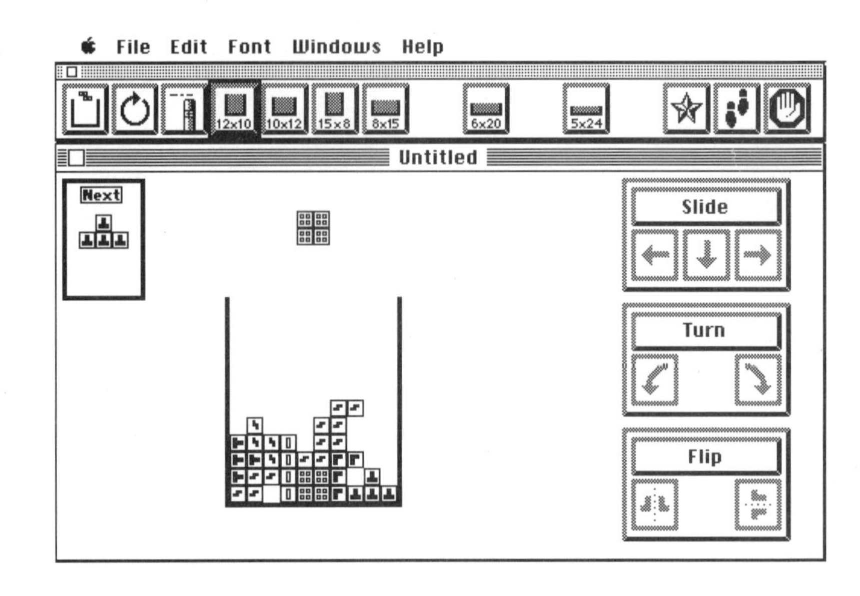

Cover the rectangle with tetrominoes.

First choose a motion: slide, flip, or turn. Then click on a button below to choose the direction of that motion.

Or use the keyboard:
S = Slide
T = Turn
F = Flip
Use the arrow keys to choose the direction.

If you choose Slide and hit the spacebar, the tetromino will drop quickly—but you can't change its direction.

Tetrominoes stick when they hit the bottom or when they hit another tetromino. If a tetromino is poking out the top of the rectangle when it sticks, it disappears.

The "Next" box shows you the next tetromino you will have to place. It can help you plan how to move so you don't leave holes.

Three different things can end the game:

- When three tetrominoes have poked out the top and disappeared, the game is over.
- Or when the rectangle is completely filled, the game is over.
- Or when you click on the Stop tool, the game is over.

Name Date

How to Play Tumbling Tetrominoes (page 2 of 2)

When the game is over, find your score. Your score is the number of squares covering the rectangle. Write the score for each game on your Game Records.

If you don't have time to finish a game, ask your teacher about saving it.

The Tool Bar

New Game Click on this to start a new game.

Replay Click on this to play your last game over again. The same tetrominoes come up in the same order.

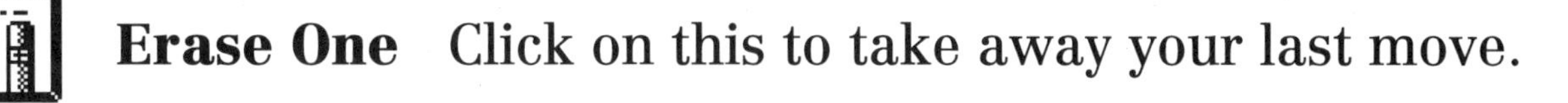

Erase One Click on this to take away your last move.

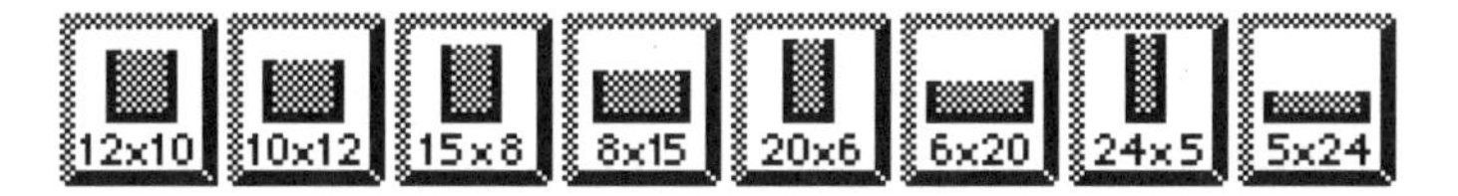

Rectangles Click on any of these to choose the shape of the rectangle you are going to cover.

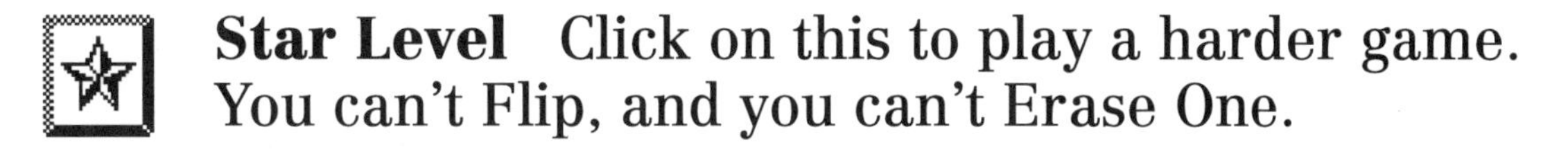

Star Level Click on this to play a harder game. You can't Flip, and you can't Erase One.

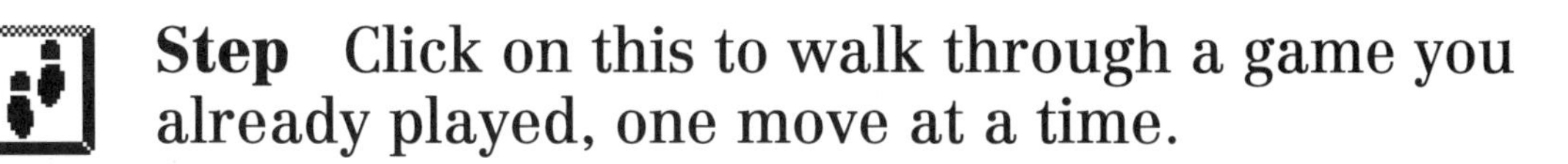

Step Click on this to walk through a game you already played, one move at a time.

Stop Click on this to end the game.

Name Date

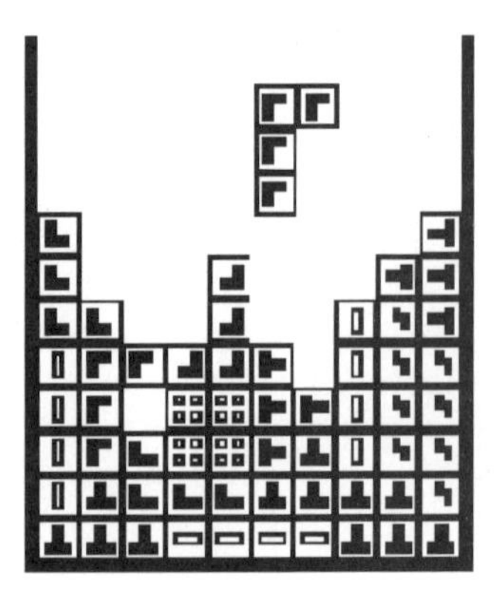

Game Records

When you play Tumbling Tetrominoes on the computer, record each game on this sheet.

In the third column, write the shape of your rectangle (for example, 10 by 12).

Game number	Date	Rectangle	Score

Name Date

Student Sheet 4

The Perfect Cover-Up

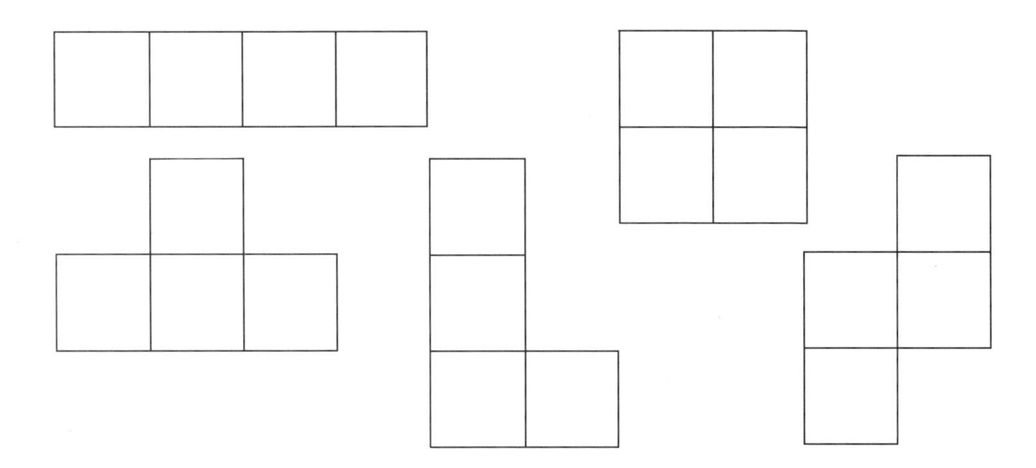

Choose one tetromino shape. Using that shape, cover as many squares as you can on the 10-by-12 Rectangle.

You can use extra copies of the 10-by-12 Rectangle to make more copies of the shape you have chosen. Or you can color in the shapes on your rectangle.

If you color each tetromino, make all the squares in one tetromino the same color. But you can use lots of colors. You could make a red tetromino, a blue tetromino, a purple tetromino, and so on.

Name Date

Student Sheet 5

How Many Squares?

Fill in the chart to show the number of total squares for each group of tetrominoes.

Number of tetrominoes	Number of squares
1	
2	
3	
4	
5	
6	
7	
8	
9	
10	
11	
12	

Suppose you had a page of 72 squares. How many of the I-shaped tetrominoes would you need to cover it?

Draw a picture to show how you solved this. Also explain in writing how you figured it out.

Name Date

Student Sheet 6

Puzzle Pieces

Which pieces fit in the holes? Draw a line from each hole in the puzzle to the piece that will fit exactly. The pieces are painted on one side only. You can't flip them. Carefully cut out the pieces. Glue in place the ones that fit.

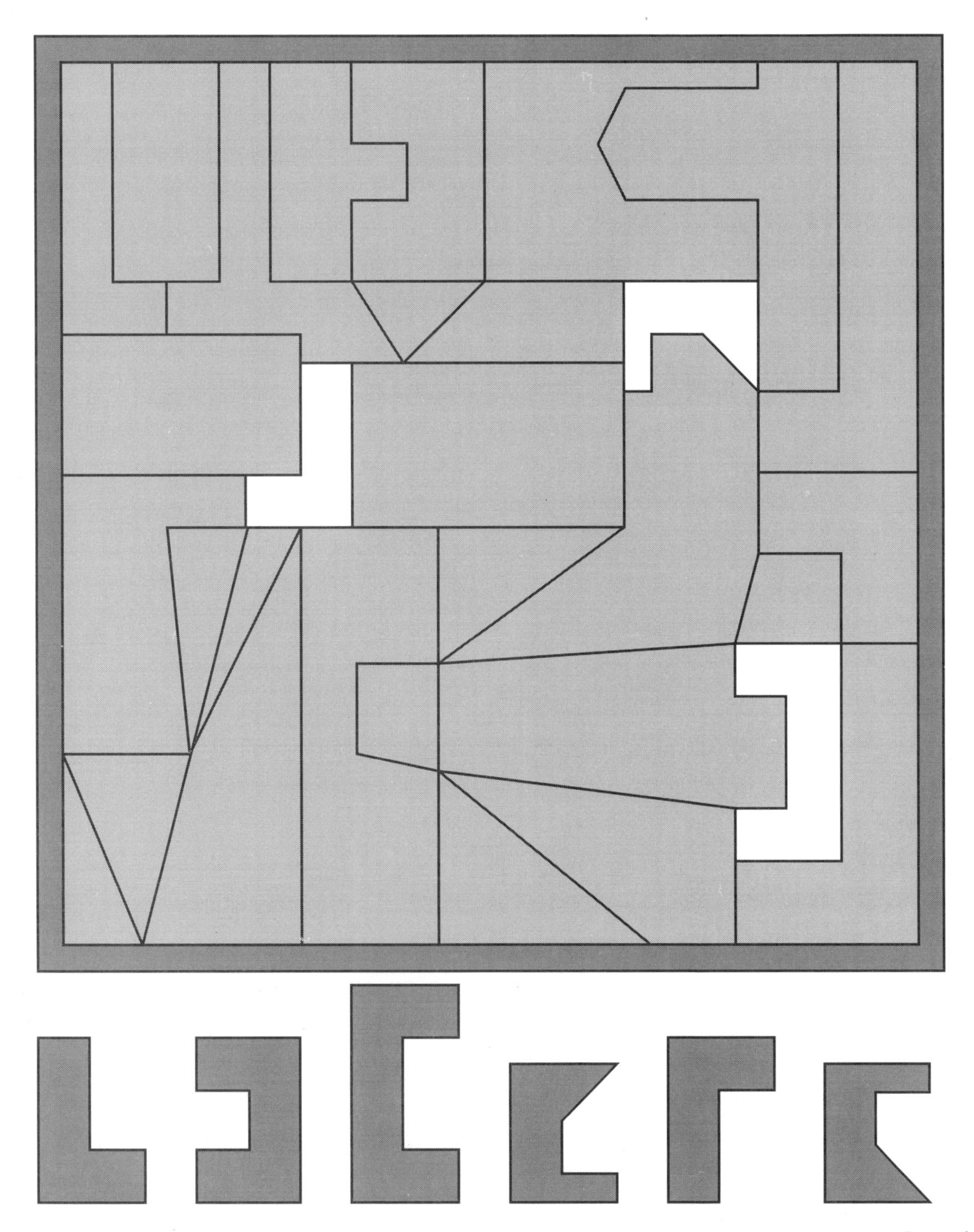

Name Date

Student Sheet 7

Tetromino Puzzle

Use this page with the Square and Triangle Cutouts.
Put together the five tetrominoes.

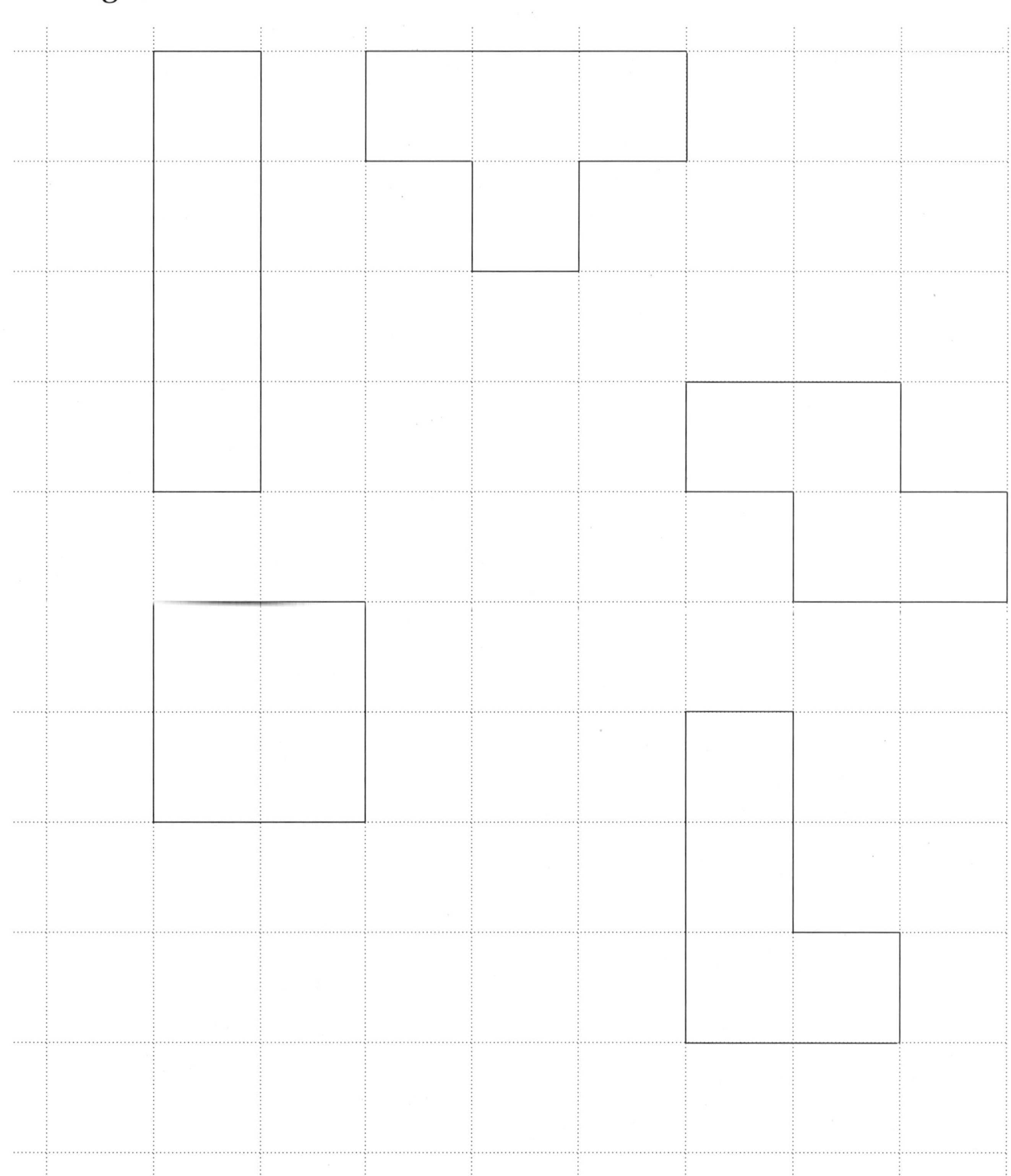

Name Date

Student Sheet 8

What's My Score?

The pictures below show three games of Tumbling Tetrominoes. For each game:

1. Figure out the total score possible.
2. Figure out the score for the game shown.

Game 1 (completed)

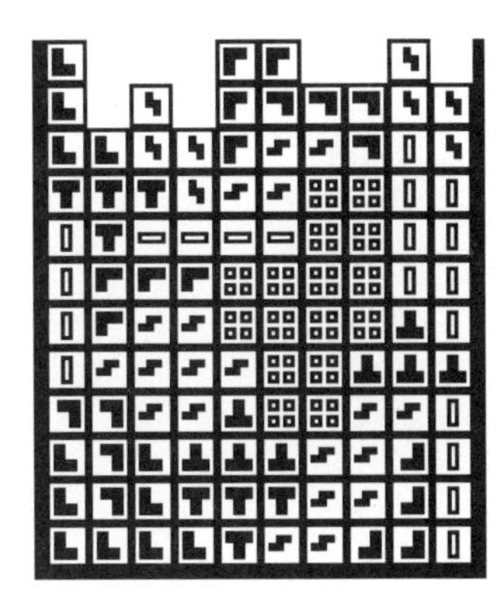

Total possible score ________

Score for this game ________

Game 2 (completed)

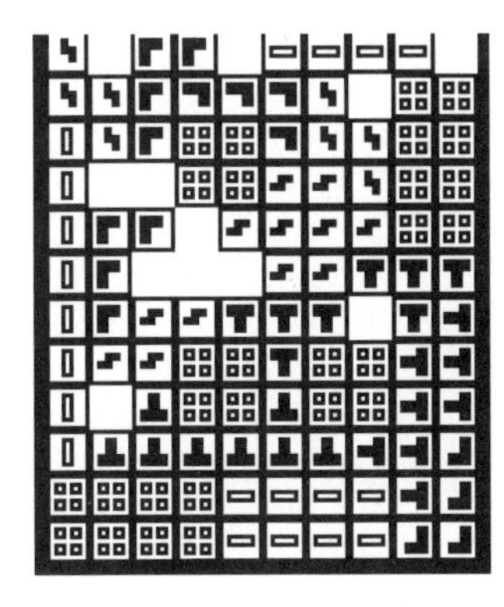

Total possible score ________

Score for this game ________

Game 3 (completed)

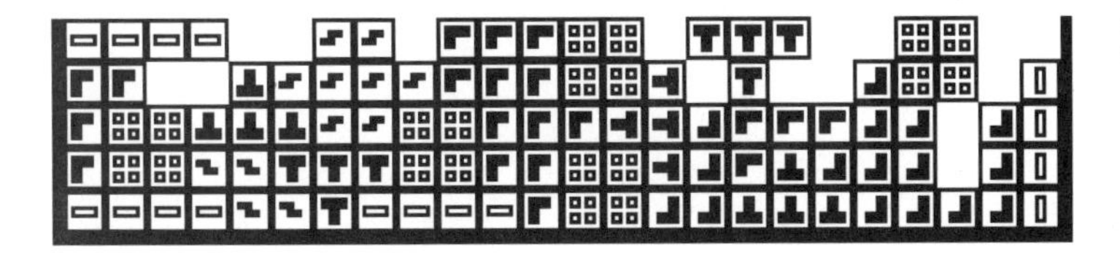

Total possible score ________

Score for this game ________

Name _______________________________ Date

Student Sheet 9

Squares! Squares! Squares!

Look around your home or neighborhood.
Find a place that is covered with squares—
maybe a floor or a ceiling.
Draw a picture of it here.

How many squares are there altogether? ______________
Did you know a way to find out how many squares **without** counting one by one? How did you do it?

____

____

____

____

____

____

Name Date

Student Sheet 10

What's My Score? What's the Area?

The pictures below show three games of Tumbling Tetrominoes. For each game:

1. Figure out the total score possible.
2. Figure out the score for the game shown.
3. Write the area of the rectangle being covered.

Game 1 (completed)

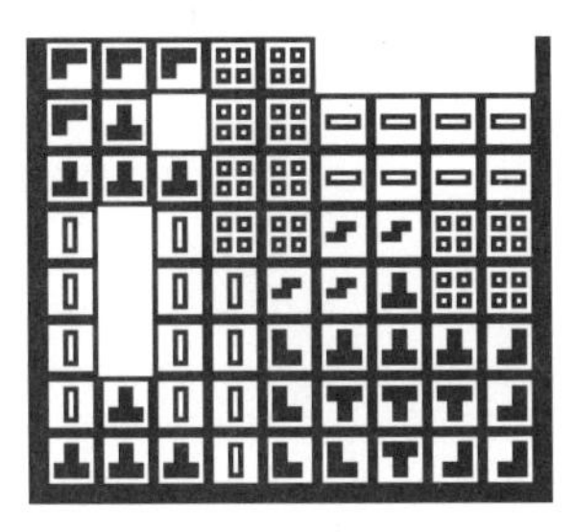

Total possible score ________

Score for this game ________

Area of rectangle ________

Game 2 (completed)

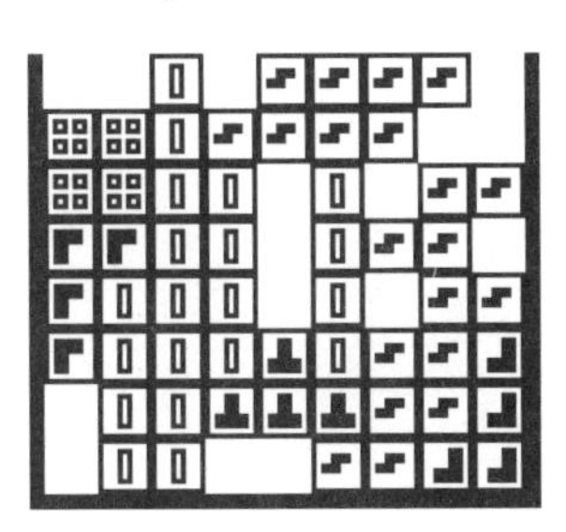

Total possible score ________

Score for this game ________

Area of rectangle ________

Game 3 (completed)

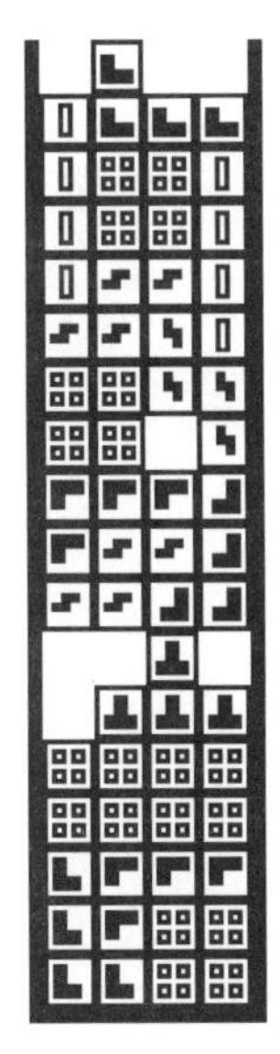

Total possible score ________

Score for this game ________

Area of rectangle ________

Name Date

Student Sheet 11

Make a Shape

Make a shape with an area of 5, 6, or 7 square units.
Draw it on the dot grid.
Use both squares and triangles in your shape.

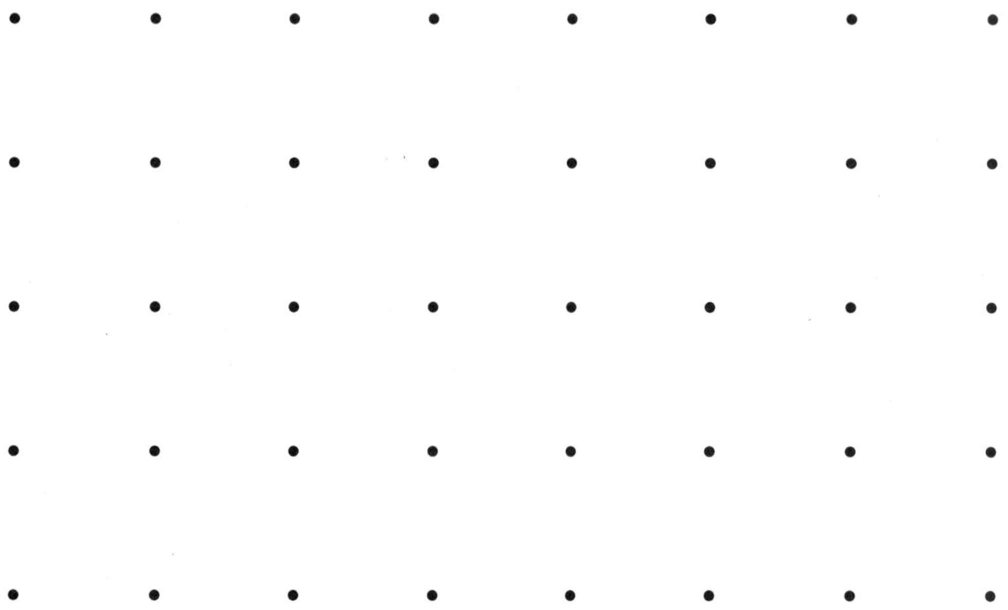

What is the area of your shape? ____________________
Write how you know your shape has that area.

Name Date

Student Sheet 12

More 4-Unit Shapes

Use the Square and Triangle Cutouts to try to make new shapes with exactly 4 square units. Remember: Each shape must, like tetrominoes, have "full sides touching."

For example, these three shapes are OK:

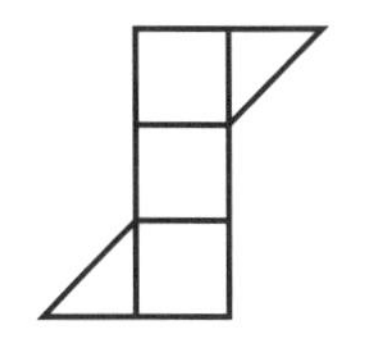

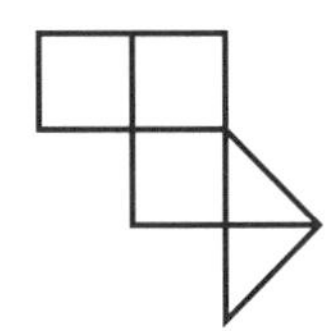

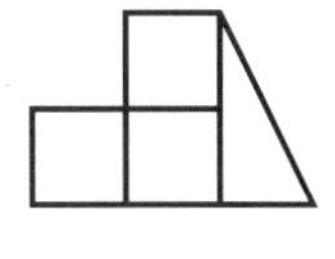

These three shapes are *not* OK (notice that some of the full sides do not match up and some of the corners are touching):

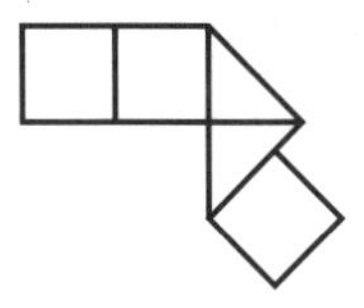

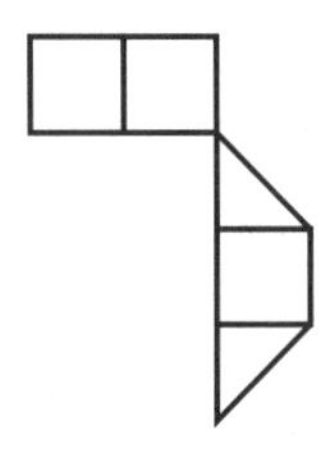

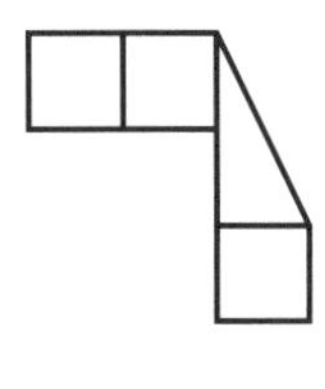

Tape or glue any new shapes you make here.

SQUARE AND TRIANGLE CUTOUTS

Cut apart all the squares and triangles on the solid lines.

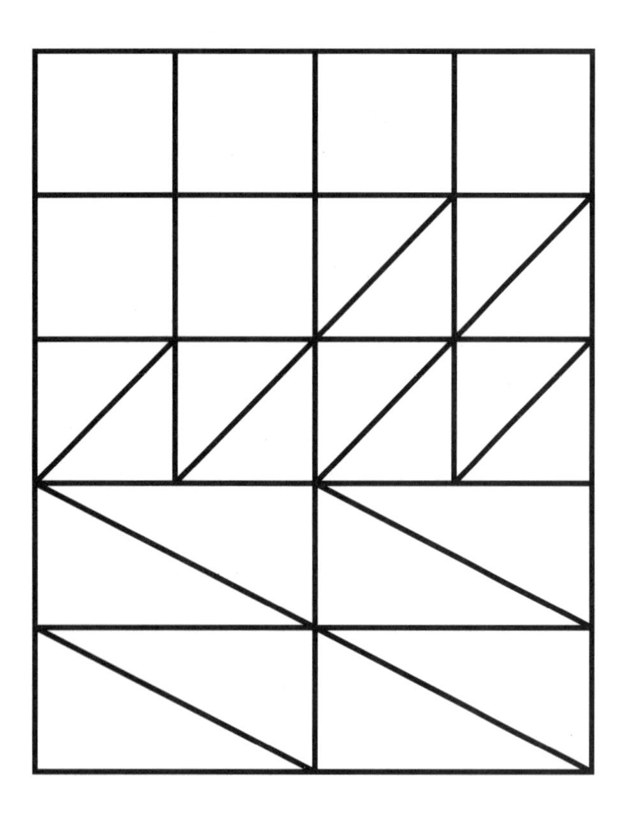

10-BY-12 RECTANGLE

Practice Pages

This optional section provides homework ideas for teachers who want or need to give more homework than is assigned to accompany the activities in this unit. The problems included here provide additional practice in learning about number relationships and in solving computation and number problems. For number units, you may want to use some of these if your students need more work in these areas or if you want to assign daily homework. For other units, you can use these problems so that students can continue to work on developing number and computation sense while they are focusing on other mathematical content in class. We recommend that you introduce activities in class before assigning related problems for homework.

The Arranging Chairs Puzzle This activity is introduced in the unit *Things That Come in Groups*. If your students are familiar with the activity, you can simply send home the directions so that students can play at home. If your students have not done this activity before, introduce it in class and have students do it once or twice before sending it home. Early in the year, ask students to work with numbers such as 15, 18, and 24. Later in the year, as they become ready to work with larger numbers, they can try numbers such as 32, 42, or 50. You might have students do this activity one time for homework in this unit.

Story Problems Story problems at various levels of difficulty are used throughout the *Investigations* curriculum. The two story problem sheets provided here help students review and maintain skills that have already been taught. You can make up other problems in this format, using numbers and contexts that are appropriate for your students. Students solve the problems and then record their strategies, using numbers, words, or pictures.

How Many Legs? This type of problem is introduced in the unit *Things That Come in Groups*. Provided here are two such problems for student homework. You can make up other problems in this format, using numbers that are appropriate for your students. Students record their strategies for solving the problems, using numbers, words, or pictures.

What You Will Need

30 small objects to use as chairs (for example, cubes, blocks, tiles, chips, pennies, buttons)

What to Do

1. Choose a number between 4 and 30.
2. Figure out all the ways you can arrange that many chairs. Each row must have the same number of chairs. Your arrangements will make rectangles of different sizes.
3. Write down the dimensions of each rectangle you make.
4. Choose another number and start again. Be sure to make a new list of dimensions for each new number.

   Example
   All the ways to arrange 12 chairs

   Dimensions
   1 by 12
   12 by 1
   2 by 6
   6 by 2
   3 by 4
   4 by 3

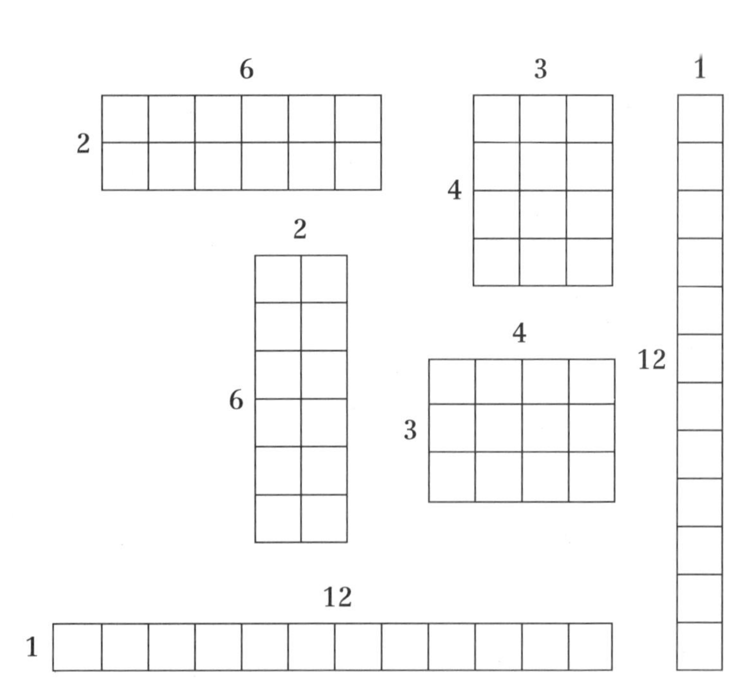

Name Date

Practice Page A

My mother bought 6 boxes of crayons. Each box had 6 crayons. How many crayons did she buy?

Show how you solved this problem. You can use numbers, words, or pictures.

Name Date

Practice Page B

My friend has 18 wood building blocks in a box. She wants to divide them equally between herself, her sister, and me. How many building blocks will we each get?

Show how you solved this problem. You can use numbers, words, or pictures.

Name Date

Practice Page C

Show how you solved each problem. You can use numbers, words, or pictures.

Dogs have 4 legs.

How many legs are on 4 dogs?

How many legs are on 8 dogs?

How many legs are on 16 dogs?

Name Date

Practice Page D

Show how you solved each problem. You can use numbers, words, or pictures.

Elephants have 2 tusks.

How many tusks are on 3 elephants?

How many tusks are on 6 elephants?

How many tusks are on 9 elephants?